THE CURRENCY

OF

THE GREAT WAR.

THE CURRENCY

OF

THE GREAT WAR

BY

BENJAMIN WHITE

(*Author of* "SILVER: ITS HISTORY AND ROMANCE," *etc.*
Fellow of the Institute of Bankers, etc.).

The Naval & Military Press Ltd

Published by

The Naval & Military Press Ltd
Unit 10 Ridgewood Industrial Park,
Uckfield, East Sussex,
TN22 5QE England

Tel: +44 (0) 1825 749494
Fax: +44 (0) 1825 765701

www.naval-military-press.com
www.nmarchive.com

In reprinting in facsimile from the original, any imperfections are inevitably reproduced and the quality may fall short of modern type and cartographic standards.

DEDICATION.

This volume is dedicated to the memory of my dear late colleagues, THOMAS EDWIN WADSWORTH *and* CHARLES EDWARD HADWEN, *both of whom were quick to obey the call of duty. They were lovely and pleasant in their lives, and in their death they were not divided in the affectionate remembrance of those who knew and loved them.*

T. E. W.	**C. E. H.**
Hetley, 8.5.1915.	Trescaut Ridge, 13.9.1918.
Aetat 19.	Aetat 39.

IN FLANDERS FIELDS.

In Flanders fields the poppies blow
Between the crosses, row on row,
   That mark our place; and in the sky
   The larks, still bravely singing, fly
Scarce heard amid the guns below.

We are the Dead. Short days ago
We lived, felt dawn, saw sunset glow,
   Loved and were loved, and now we lie
      In Flanders fields.

Take up our quarrel with the foe:
To you from failing hands we throw
   The torch; be yours to hold it high.
   If ye break faith with us who die
We shall not sleep, though poppies grow
      In Flanders fields.

Dr. John McCrae,
With the forces Overseas.

Lieutenant=Colonel McCrae
now lies amid the poppies—he died January 28th, 1918.

Let us never pass by the need of any who took the sacred flame from those dead hands!

The above poem is used by kind permission of the proprietors of Punch.

PREFACE.

WHEN the Day of Visitation dawned on the memorable Fourth of August, 1914, the writer—like most men over military age—was alert for opportunities of humble service. At evening time he sought to hearten the lads from farm, factory and desk, who, dressed in civilian clothes, marched about the hills of Eastbourne in September, 1914, but, to his surprise, found that they, not he, imparted the good cheer. Alas! how many of them have paid the great sacrifice, or—what often has been more painful—have had to live, maimed and infirm, ill-fitted for the strenuous struggle for existence.

These brave souls were the germ of an organism, ultimately numbering five million, who voluntarily risked their all for Home and Country—an effort unsurpassed in the History of the World.

Did the heroic dead, and the no less heroic living, suffer in vain? The Psalmist of old declared: "He that goeth forth and weepeth, bearing precious seed, should doubtless come again with rejoicing, bringing his sheaves with him." They were indeed *precious seed*, culled from the finest flower of the Nation! The husbandman ever selects the choicest material for sowing, and all religious tenets without exception demand the very best for sacrifice. The bloom of youth, the charm of physical health, the rich endowment of clear brain power and high courage sowed the plains of Flanders, the cliffs of Gallipoli, the defiles of the Jordan Valley, the swamps of East Africa, the torrid wastes of Mesopotamia, and many another hallowed spot, not forgetting the ocean bed.

Make no mistake. Choice seed like this will germinate in due time—or the very laws of the Universe must come to grief. We see now through a glass darkly—political unrest, and industrial strife, obscure the vision. The state of nervous tension endured for five dread years of awful strain can relax only with time and palliative measures. When the body politic regains health and tone, shame will be the portion of those members who have yielded to the claims of self, and have forgotten the gracious memory, or ignored the honourable wounds of those who bore the burden of the fray.

The following extract from an article upon the function of gold in international finance published in the *Bankers' Magazine* of April, 1916, was penned by the author during some of the darkest days of the War, and may here be fitly reproduced:—

"As to what will be the credit of the British Empire amongst the nations of the World after the war, there is no reason to imagine that it will be diminished. The burden of financing her great allied nations has fallen upon her shoulders. The bonds of trade between the Allies will be forged closer, and it will be done in Great Britain's workshops. If the British nation were effete and decadent, there might be some reason to fear that hands, which tried in vain to snatch the trident from its grasp, might rob it of its financial crown. But the fact that four or five million of the British race voluntarily have flown to arms in order to defend their heritage gives to such an insinuation the lie direct. The British race is still virile, and the world will not be discouraged from leaving its balances in London, when it reflects that London's sons have shed their blood willingly in Flanders to maintain the honour and credit of British plighted word.

"British banking will not attract less confidence abroad when it is found that the shock of the greatest war the world has ever seen has not disturbed its equilibrium. A liner in foreign ports flying the British flag will be none the less welcome because the British Navy will have crushed a revival of piracy upon the main, and by so doing will have secured the freedom of the seas to all peaceful traders.

"The financial future of London and its power to maintain a free flow of gold are not unconnected with the fact that the Empire produces each year about double as much gold as the rest of the world, but a supply of gold alone will not suffice. The crying need, in this great crisis of British history, is for statesmen, who, placing patriotism before party, shall initiate measures by which British trade can be guided, and stimulated to a degree commensurate with the vast resources of the Empire. Nevertheless, after all, the decision of this great question lies in the avoidance by the British Nation of a sloth arising from prosperity or of a slough of materialism, in both of which lurks the germ of decay. The economist no less than the moralist views the sifting of nations during the last twenty months as a lesson to be turned to profit. Sound honest trading is the key to success, and if the British race accept the chastening of the Great War as for their good, they will lift up the hands which hang down, and strengthen the feeble knees and make straight paths for their feet, and the future outstretches full of hope even for their children's children."

The illustrations are taken from a collection in the writer's possession, for most of which he is indebted to the kindness of friends who took an interest in what is at present an uncommon line of research. No attempt has been made to make the survey complete, the range is far too wide for such a modest work as this. Enough, however, is presented to give the reader some idea of the way in which the Great World Crisis upheaved currency conventions, in like manner as it dealt radically with almost every other department of human activity.

PREFACE.

The chapters represent eight articles published at irregular intervals in the *Bankers' Magazine*. The letterpress remains substantially unaltered, notwithstanding that the bulk was written during the heat of conflict. Base counterfeits of what is Right, Noble, and Just—the finest human currency—should, like false coin, be nailed to the counter as a warning to posterity, even though the utterer has paid the penalty.

Grateful acknowledgment is due to a number of joint stock banks, private firms and individuals who have given advance orders for sufficient copies to defray the cost of printing a first edition, and by so doing have ensured a certain contribution to the Blinded Soldiers' and Sailors' Hostel, commonly known as St. Dunstan's, to which the entire profits are devoted.

Messrs. Waterlow & Sons Limited (who own the copyright of the words and of the beautifully produced illustrations) have generously granted the use of them for the purpose of this work.

BENJAMIN WHITE.

December, 1920.

CONTENTS.

CHAPTER I.
War Currency in Enemy Countries 1

CHAPTER II.
Emergency War Money Issued in France 9

CHAPTER III.
More Enemy War Currency 25

CHAPTER IV.
Belgian War Currency 41

CHAPTER V.
Russian War Currency 59

CHAPTER VI.
Allied War Emergency Money 75

CHAPTER VII.
Neutral War Emergency Money 89

CHAPTER VIII.
British War Emergency Money 97

LIST OF ILLUSTRATIONS.

	PAGE.
AALST—25 c.	47
AISNE AND ARDENNES—25 c.	28
AVEYRON—50 c.	19
BAD KREUZNACH—50 pf., obverse	29
,, reverse	29
BELGIAN BANQUE NATIONALE—5 fr.	42
,, ,, —2 fr.	43
,, ,, —1 fr.	43
POOR RELIEF NOTE	49
SOCIÉTÉ GÉNÉRALE—1 fr., obverse	44
,, ,, ,, reverse	44
,, ,, —20 fr.	49
BÉZIERS—1 fr.	17
BINCHE—10 c.	51
BRUGGE (BRUGES)—25 c.	47
CARTONS—FRENCH	13
COINS—BELGIAN	40
FRENCH	11
GERMAN	24
GERMAN EAST AFRICA	33
SCANDINAVIA	88
CRACOW—½ korony	95
DARLEHENKASSENSCHEIN—1 mk., obverse	1
,, reverse	2
DENMARK—1 krone	91
ELENE, 25 c.	56
FRENCH ASSIGNAT—125 livre	68
FÜSSEN (GERMAN MICHAEL)—50 pf.	30
GERMAN EAST AFRICAN NOTE—1 rupee	36
5 rupee	37
1 rupee (Packing Paper)	38
IMPERIAL—20 mk.	Frontispiece
MICHAEL—reverse (FÜSSEN NOTE), 50 pf.	30
GLOGAU—½ mk.	35
GORLITZ—50 pf., obverse	31
,, reverse	31
GREECE—1 drachma	84
2 drachma	84
GROUP—70 FRENCH COMMUNES	19
HOLLAND—2½ gulden	93
ITALIAN—2 lire	76
JAPANESE—50 sen	85
JAROTSCHIN—2 mk.	6
LEUVEN (LOUVAIN)—10 c.	54

	PAGE
LOUVAIN (LEUVEN)—25 c.	45
MALINES—10 c.	53
50 c.	53
MILOSLAW—5 mk.	5
MOUSCRON—10 c., obverse	48
,, reverse	48
NIEDERLAHNSTEIN—50 pf., obverse	26
,, reverse	26
25 pf., obverse	27
OSTEND—25 c.	47
PRINCE PLESS'S WORKS—1 mk.	3
QUIEVRAIN—25 c	48
ROSTOFF s/DON—5 rouble	61
10 rouble	70
25 rouble	70
100 rouble	58
ROUMANIA—2 lei	80
5 lei	81
5 lei in enemy occupation	81
25 bani	83
50 bani	83
ROUVEROY—10 c.	48
RUSSIA—1 kopeck	60
1, 2, 3, 10, 15, 20 kopeck (stamp design)	60
IRON COIN, 3 kopeck	60
ARCHANGEL, 10 roubles	63
BRITISH ARCHANGEL, 1 rouble	67
DARLEHENKASSENSCHEIN, 1 rouble	62
,, 2 rouble	63
KERENSKY, 40 rouble, reverse	72
,, ,, obverse	72
SAARBRUCKEN—50 pf.	32
SERVIA—5 dinar	74
SOIGNIES—10 c.	56
SWEDEN—1 krone	91
SWITZERLAND—5 fr.	93
TIENEN (TIRLEMONT)—10 c.	54
TIRLEMONT (TIENEN)—10 c	54
TOULOUSE—1 fr.	17
TREPORT—25 c.	19
UDINE—1 lire	77
UNTERGUTSCH—SHOP	7
VENETIA—5 c.	79
1 lira	74
2 lira	77
VERVIERS—25 c.	52
VEZON—25 c.	55
VILLE D'ATH—25 c.	55
VLADIVOSTOK—50 kopeck	66
WARSAW—1 mk.	95
WILSELE—2 c.	46
WITTEN—SAVINGS BANK, 50 pf.	4

s imprint of an invocation to the Great Arbiter of the Universe upon an Imperial German Note is, like the Hymn of Hate, a remarkable revelation of German mentality.

CHAPTER I.

WAR CURRENCY IN ENEMY COUNTRIES.

FAILING the production of those State Papers, which eventually must see the light and pin the guilt for the catastrophe which befell the world over four years ago upon its wicked authors for ever, the currency note here illustrated is a useful piece of circumstantial evidence. A button, or some such trivial clue, has often been the means of bringing a criminal to expiate his sin upon the scaffold. In such wise this Mark note, elaborate in design, printed in three colours, issued by an organisation *which had no existence* prior to

August, 1914, is damning evidence that the crime was conceived and pre-arranged as to the minutest detail long before it was perpetrated. Loan Banks, described as Darlehenskassen, were instituted almost immediately after the outbreak of war, for the express purpose of granting credit upon the security of property. Much of this property, from its very nature, could not be profit-earning, and a good deal must soon have ceased to be so after war began. Without any doubt, in not a few cases, some of the latter will never resume that function.

It is not surprising that Germany, about to traverse a path, suspended upon financial planks so slender and so ill-secured across a fateful future, should have sought to hearten its people with the vision of a massive bridge based upon War Indemnities, and should have deemed its attainment to be of vital necessity to her future economic existence.

These notes formed an important part of War Finance, for they were decreed by legislative enactment, when held by the Reichsbank, to be reckoned equally with gold, as cover for the Reichsbank's own notes.

The date of the specimen illustrated—August 12, 1914—is worthy of attention, for it invites us to compare its artistic workmanship with that of the British Currency note, first issued on August 7, 1914. No one who examines an original Bradbury can doubt that its design

and execution were hastily improvised. This German note, on the contrary, bears upon its face clear indication that it was a carefully devised cog-wheel in the mechanism of the infernal machine suddenly hurled with such dire effect amongst the peaceful nations of Europe.

To an uncanny extent, a mist of exceeding density had shrouded the actual conditions of life in Germany from our ken. Signals of distress were occasionally wafted from the lesser conspirators against the world's liberty, but, up to a recent date, the arch-malefactor, with a certain rugged majesty, had moved toward his doom, with the assertion that all was well and must be well, because of an unshakable will to victory. The fog had seemed to lift occasionally when a neutral emerged from the obscured region, bearing tidings of good or evil, as his sympathy or range of observation might direct, but, in order to gauge the situation, particularly the economic condition of the German Empire, incontestable and tangible evidence has been the desideratum as proof beyond cavil. Such is to be obtained from the succeeding illustrations.

One aspect of the difficulties that German commerce has had to face in regard to finance is disclosed by the second of the notes. The Prince of Pless owns certain works near his castle of Waldenburg. Doubtless, soon after the beginning of war, he approached his bankers for the customary facilities necessary to finance his undertakings. His mines had instantly been set hard at work on behalf of the Government, from whom, in due course, payment would eventually be received. The bankers, it is reasonable to infer, felt unable to comply. In days gone by they had had no difficulty in providing

---

Nr. 4404
Gutschein über 1 Mk.
in Worten: Eine Mark.
Fürstlich Plessische Bergwerks-Direktion
zu Schloss Waldenburg.

Ungültig

Dieser Gutschein wird bis zum 20. Oktober 1914 von der Fürstlichen Grubenkasse und vom Fürstlichen Warenhause eingelöst.

---

the Prince with funds, for they had been in the habit of discounting either his bills, or bills of similar Trading Concerns, in the most favourable quarter for such a purpose, the one always at the service of friendly commercial communities in good repute, namely, the London Money Market. This practice, as regards the industrial concerns of Germany, has probably come to an end.

The agents of the Prince of Pless solved the problem by paying workmen, and possibly tradesmen as well, in notes which pledged the credit of his undertakings. The notes state that they are cashable at the Princely treasuries, and at the Princely stores. Having been issued in denominations as high as ten marks, they seem to have been an adroit solution of the Princely difficulties, arising in the course of the Princely business. It will be observed that the note illustrated has been duly cashed; considering, however, that finance has not improved in Germany since the due date of the note—October 20, 1914—it was probably cashed in fresh paper, together with its brethren.

The third note is not of a comforting description for persons of a saving disposition. Though this note is valued for only fifty pfennige, similar notes are known to be in existence of a much

higher denomination. They represent all that many poor folk have to show for their hardly earned savings, of which their Government has probably assumed charge after taking the funds out of the hands of the institution to which they were originally committed. The note has doubtless been cashed in paper currency of imperial or local issue; if in the latter, substantial depreciation is bound to have taken place, as against Government issues possessing unrestricted legal tender.

Many notes issued by Prussian towns and other authorities bear a time limit—December 31, 1914. This date seems to echo the King of Prussia's confident prediction to his legions in 1914, to the effect that their victorious return was assured *before the fall of the leaf*.

The fourth note comes somewhat as a shock to the eye of a banker. Money is such a serious matter, that, to tear a sheet of notepaper into four pieces, to use a typewriter to add value for four marks, to back the inscription with a town stamp and a signature, both imposed with the aid of a rubber stamp, savours of sacrilege. So simple an effort to create money must have induced many amateur and unofficial note manufacturers to enter into competition with the authorities.

The fifth note dispenses with all mechanical aid, save that of a rubber stamp bearing the badge of the town. In the case of this

note the method of production seems to have been somewhat of this fashion. A deputation informed the Burgomaster that local supplies of currency had disappeared, and proposed that he should make an issue on behalf of the town. Like his colleague already mentioned, he tore some of his notepaper into four pieces, upon each of which he wrote the numeral 2, signed his name, and imprinted the town's seal. Some stander-by suggested that a little information, as to what the "2" indicated, would be useful. The different hand in which the words "good for" and the letter "M" are written, as well as the fact that they show signs of having been promptly blotted, suggest that his reply was "don't bother *me*—fill in yourself what you think is necessary."

The last note relates to the Austrian Empire, and has been issued by a tradesman. Harassed as shopkeepers may be in this country by Government regulations and the importunities of their customers, they have not been able to compensate themselves by issuing currency of their own, as this gentleman has done, whose varied business embraces groceries, colonial goods, dyes and delicatessen. The last expression, in these hard times, is of dubious and somewhat ominous import. Doubtless many a poor person changed

an imperial krone note at his shop, and received in exchange a piece of blood sausage, and 80 heller in cardboard notes of this design. There must have come a time when other tradesmen in the town began to look with jealous eye upon the extent to which Herr Untergutsch employed the local printing press in order to further his business, and began to insist upon a discount before receiving his currency into their own tills. In a word, every merchant's notes are bound to depreciate before long, when applied to other purchases than those at the issuer's shop. The matter must have become serious indeed for consumers. The poor populace, not the tradesman, is the helpless party, for every shopkeeper has the power to safeguard himself by *raising the price* of his commodities, in correspondence with the *falling value* of his currency.

The design of camel and pyramids, figured on the reverse of Herr Untergutsch's note, may be a reminder to his customers that the victory of the Austrian arms would enable them to receive from Egypt (replaced under the Turkish yoke), and *viâ* the Balkan Zug, her choicest products.

The amount of paper currency possessing imperial sanction and circulating in Germany exceeded, in September, 1918, 1,200 million pounds sterling in nominal value. The specimens of other paper

Schutzmarke.

currency, of which only a few illustrations have been here presented, afford an indication, necessarily slight but none the less certain, that, in addition to this huge amount, there is circulating in enemy countries an enormous quantity of notes based upon private credit, the existence of which is fraught with danger and certain misery to their people. An examination of varieties issued by other towns and by mining companies, etc., shows that no apparent limit has been set to the extent of these issues, which, in most instances, are not even numbered. When the effect of military defeat is felt to the full, the chance of local credit surviving the coming shock, which will shake national credit to its very root, is very faint, and the condition of poor folk, who have the misfortune to hold these scraps of paper, will be pitiable indeed.

The world may yet have to look on, with bated breath, whilst the befooled inhabitants of enemy countries settle with their erstwhile rulers, who, in a wild gamble for world domination, have sacrificed the blood of millions of their subjects, have squandered the property and savings of most of the remainder, and have pawned for many years to come the labour of their hands.

Since the above lines were penned, a short month ago, the march of retribution has been so swift, and the drama on the World's stage has proceeded with such fell intent, that the events foreshadowed in the concluding paragraph have materialised into stern fact.

The above, written a fortnight before the Armistice, first appeared in print at the beginning of December, 1918.

CHAPTER II.

EMERGENCY WAR MONEY ISSUED IN FRANCE.

WE who, notwithstanding our proximity to the late arena of war, have been fortunate enough to be sheltered from the fierce shocks which have fallen upon our French allies, have but a dim perception of the straits to which they have been exposed. With them we have shared a certain degree of danger from hostile military action, and we have undergone the chastening consequent upon a serious increase in the cost of the necessaries of life, but, whatever trials we have had to undergo, we have not had to face the possibility of a hostile occupation of our capital, nor have we felt the severity of economic pressure arising from a deficiency of the baser metals—circumstances which have dealt hardly with our gallant Ally.

Toward the close of 1914 the invader was almost knocking at the gates of Paris, and those steps which common prudence dictated, at once were taken to provide against any break in the continuity of the industries commonly practised in the French capital. One of the precautions was to move the Mint to a safer locality. With this end in view, its operations were transferred to Castelsarrasin, a town situated in the Department of Tarn et Garonne, much farther off than Paris from the military zone. Silver coins of the denominations of one and two francs which were struck in this town during the temporary sojourn of the Mint are imprinted with the letter **C** upon the reverses. Such is the eagerness of coin collectors to secure this evidence of the imminent danger faced by the French capital that they are willing to pay ten francs for the former and eight francs for the latter. Both of these coins are reproduced on the accompanying plate.

The almost insatiable appetite of the guns so denuded the country of copper and nickel that it became impossible to provide money composed of those materials in quantity sufficient to meet the demand for currency, augmented as it was by the presence of great masses of troops and by the diversion of trade to new channels. Hence various authorities (municipalities, chambers of commerce, mines, etc.) were empowered to issue subsidiary coins for use in their localities. In some few cases these coins were struck in copper, such as those circulated by the Nouvelle Galeries at Bordeaux, the town of Coueron (Loire Inf.), Digoin, Lyon, Ouveillan and Toulouse.

Brass was selected by Digoin as material for a ten-franc piece, and by Bone (Algeria) for denominations of a franc and a half franc. As a rule, however, it was employed by towns and cities for the smaller fractions of a franc; amongst such places were Chaton, Givors, La Rochelle, Mazamet, Montpellier, Nantes, Ouveillan, Toulouse and Unieux.

A decided preference was shown for the use of aluminium. This is not surprising when the light specific gravity of the metal is considered, though, from a numismatic point of view, other metals take a more satisfactory impression. Amongst the towns favouring this medium were Besançon, Billancourt, Blois, Bompas, Bone (Algeria), Bougie (Algeria), Carcassonne, Carmaux, Castres (Tarn), Courneuve, Damiatte, Digoin, Gard, Le Havre, Issoire, Joinville-le-Pont, La Rochelle (Tramways), Laroque d'Holmes, Malakoff, Marseille, Montpellier, Nantes (Les Boulangers), Narbonne, Neuilly-sur-Seine, Perpignan, Poissy, Rochefort-sur-Mer, Rouen, St. Germain-en-laye, Saint Sulpice, Thiviers, Unieux, Vanves and Vincennes. The use of aluminium for money may have served as a memento that the enemy Zeppelins, composed largely of this metal, had failed in their terrorising object. Three specimens of these—two circular varieties issued by Marseilles and an unusual shaped coin of Carcassonne— have been selected for illustration.

Zinc also enjoyed some popularity. Coins were struck in this material by Alger (Ch. de C.), Bourg, Carmaux, Castelnaudary, Cette, Digoin, Gueugnon, Herault, Le Puy, Lyon, Narbonne, Perpignan, Region Provençale, Sail-sous-Couzan, Saint Sulpice and Versailles. Of these coins, those issued by Bourg, Digoin, Sail-sous-Couzan and Saint Sulpice were coated with nickel. None of the zinc pieces shown in the illustration is of impressive design

Iron was utilised by Albi (Tarn), Bayonne, Bordeaux, Pau, Tarbes and Valentigney. The coins of the first named are *tinned*, somewhat after the principle of the domestic saucepan.

It will be observed that the town of Digoin was exceptionally enterprising. Its issues comprise coins formed respectively of four

FRENCH CARTON EMERGENCY MONEY

different metals: copper, zinc, aluminium and brass. The varieties of these metal coins or tokens circulating in France and Algeria exceed one hundred in number.

A far greater number of local authorities decided to issue small pieces of cardboard in lieu of metal discs. In some instances, such as those circulated in Beaumont de Lomagne and Grenade (arr. de Toulouse), the edges are protected with metal.

It would naturally be supposed that the bulk of this new description of money would imitate the circular shape of a coin. This is not the case; the variety of outline is quite remarkable, as will be seen by glancing at the second plate accompanying this article. Amongst the specimens represented, special interest attaches to the circlet, over-printed with olive green, which did service for 5 centimes in the district of Lille. It calls to mind the occupation and ill treatment by the enemy of the long-suffering inhabitants of this important industrial centre.

Square pieces of cardboard were generally favoured, such as the 5-centime denomination issued by the Société des Aceries et Forges at Firminy (Loire). This institution differentiated by shape the value of each token. The 10-centime piece is round and the 25-centime hexagonal. The reverse of each denomination bears an inscription that they are encashable up to December 31, 1920, for 1 franc in exchange for four 25-centime, ten 10-centime or twenty 5-centime pieces. The town of Caussade (Tarn et Garonne) possessed an octagon 5-centime piece, whilst Le Havre (Trefileries et Laminoirs) circulated rectangular 5 and 10-centime pieces with rounded corners. Some of the cartons are coated with gelatine, but most are of undressed cardboard.

Tradesmen—grocers, bakers, drapers, milkmen, butchers, barbers, chemists, restaurateurs, coal merchants, druggists and motor owners—all entered upon the novel industry of supplying the public with cardboard cash, as well as many folk, well-known doubtless in their locality, who did not find it necessary to advertise the nature of their business on their tokens.

Municipalities and rural boards were responsible for the greater number of tokens, but companies relating to mines, tramways, water, electricity and steel works, etc., consulted their own and their employees' convenience by providing these useful temporary substitutes for metal coin.

Some of the cartons are of quite pleasing design, particularly the series (printed in a warm brown tint) for circulation by the Union Commerciale of Brive, in the Department of Corrèze. This town, the ancient Briva Curretia, derives its name from an old Celtic word for bridge. It pursues an active trade in early vegetables and fruit, grain, livestock and truffles, produced in the rich valley where it is situated. The dignified female head and bust, which adorns the carton in the illustration, wears the head-dress styled "Barbichet Limousin," which is distinctive of the district. The engraver of the carton, himself a native of Brive, selected a young lady of the town for his model, and has since made her his wife. He has thus made her an historic personage as well as his bride.

The very public themselves seem to have entered into organised participation, for 5, 10, 25 and 50-centime pieces were put into circulation by a body possessing this high-sounding title: "The Restaurant Customers' Union of the Western Suburbs of Paris."

Notes, some of considerable artistic design, were issued by chambers of commerce and other authorities for denominations of 25 centimes and upwards. Most of these bear an inscription somewhat to the following effect: This note, guaranteed by the deposit of an equal sum at the Bank of France, is exchangeable against notes of the Bank of France in the district if presented before such and such a date.

The first of the notes illustrated is of somewhat elaborate design executed in faint blue and pink. The second is bold and striking in appearance with bands of black and vermilion. The issue of money by local authorities bearing the name of the town or district in which they were intended to circulate must have helped to make it popular, appealing as it did to local pride as well as patriotism. The love which a man bears to the place of his birth, or to the locality where his forbears have tilled the soil and been interred, is no faint emotion. The seated statue of Strasbourg, in the Place de Concorde in Paris, swathed in sable and hung with mourning wreaths for some fifty years, has been clear evidence of that. The time will come when the need for emergency currency shall have passed away, and the financial wounds of France shall be healed, but, for many generations to come, specimens of this local currency will be treasured as a memento of the great tribulation through which France emerged triumphant.

FRENCH EMERGENCY NOTES

FRENCH EMERGENCY NOTES

The last note illustrated is of touching interest. It was issued by a group of townships and villages which had combined together for the purpose. Printed in black upon grey paper, it suggests by its sombre design the dire experiences of the district in which it was intended to circulate. The piece of paper typifies the indomitable spirit of France; that ethereal, incalculable quality which has utterly defeated the utmost brute force which the Germans could bring to bear. It bears impressed upon it names which stir the blood, and will ever stir the blood of the French and British nations alike. They tell of heroic deeds and desperate struggles in which the sons of these two races stood shoulder to shoulder. Seventy names of towns and hamlets which guarantee the notes are recorded in minute lettering within a space less than two inches long by half an inch broad. The surge of battle swung to and fro until nothing was left to mark the sites of some of these once prosperous communities—but mounds of ruins and heaps of dead.

What names! Miraumont, Courcelette, Ligny, Warlencourt, Avesnes, Le Transloy, Sailly Sallisel, Bapaume, Achiet-le-Petit, Martinpuich. *Quelle glorieuse monnaie! Vive la France.*

GERMAN LOCAL MONEY.

CHAPTER III.

MORE ENEMY WAR CURRENCY.

THE scarcity of those base metals commonly employed for the lowest grades of coinage has been felt acutely in Germany, where local production could not be supplemented by supplies drawn from overseas, owing to the cordon which sea power had set about the Central Empires. Nothing was more natural than that, when savagery and lust broke loose and carnage encrimsoned copse and countryside, and when supplies of copper and nickel ran short, recourse should be made to that metal which forms part of the familiar German phrase, "Blood and Iron." Hence Germany was prompt to use this metal for Imperial ten and five pfennig pieces. Iron had previously served a similar purpose in Germany during the period of the Napoleonic Wars.

Towns followed suit and issued currency in this metal, which, however well fitted for the purpose in respect of its hardness, is very unsuitable from its tendency to corrosion. Amongst such local authorities were the towns of Bonn and Duren.

Germany had drawn freely from the practically unlimited metallic resources of the British Empire in pre-war days—so freely that it had obtained a monopoly of the mineral wealth of Australia (particularly that of zinc) by methods considered somewhat slim. This metal has been employed during the war for the provision of Imperial and local ten pfennig and other pieces. The former bear on the reverse the familiar design embodying the Imperial eagle with outspread wings, symbolical of great ambition, and displaying huge talons, ready to prey with relentless grasp. The local coins mostly simulate the plain clear obverse of the Imperial coin, with value expressed in numerals, whilst the reverse bears a shield or other token of local significance. Of such a character are the ten and five pfennig pieces of Duren, Boltrop, Bonn, Witten, Landkrels Lennep, Bingen Rhein, Elberfeld, Sinzig, as here illustrated.

OBVERSE

REVERSE

So surpassingly strange have been the vicissitudes of the last five years that any thread is of real value that can enable us to trace the inwardness of the momentous events that have taken place. With this end in view, historians will delve for many future decades amongst multitudinous documents, and will, in course of time, unravel the baffled plot against the peace of the world and the rights of humanity at large. Not the least interesting line of research will be the amazing mentality of the would-be Dictators of the Universe. Some of the illustrations which accompany this article, dealing though it does with so prosaic a subject as currency, will be found to throw some light upon the remarkable composition of the

German temperament. From it, have been evolved qualities that would adorn Lucifer himself, such as boundless ambition and the ruthless employment of any means, fair or foul, in order to compass a desired end! We hope and trust that these evil traits, largely owing to calculated cultivation by wicked counsellors, may be eliminated, and that its finer qualities, precision and thoroughness, industry and domesticity, may ultimately restore the German nation to the esteem of its fellows.

A note issued by the town of Niederlahnstein reveals a homely wit, combined with an absence of personal dignity, which is in strange contrast to the awful pass to which the German nation has been brought.

If the illustration of the reverse of the note be examined with care, it will be observed that each of the small circlets on the obverse and reverse contain the name of the town " Stadt Niederlahnstein " issuing this paper money, with two exceptions, namely, those just above the ham and above the swedes or turnips, which are portrayed on the reverse. The words above the ham run thus:—" Zarte sehnsucht susses hoffen," a line from Schiller, which may be translated, " tender longing, sweet hopes," whilst above the swedes is a line from an old German song, " So leben wir, so leben wir," meaning " thus we live, thus we live." In the grave circumstances, the imprint of a jest upon the very currency itself betrays an abnormal condition of mind—a flippancy and lack of self-respect.

The German Government disapproved of this note and ordered it to be recalled. The specimen here reproduced cost fifteen shillings; the rarity of the note will probably lead to a much higher fancy value.

Another note issued by the same town is here represented. The design seems to be intended as humorous, but according to the canons of British taste can only be described as gross and vulgar. Attention appears to be drawn to the inflation of the currency and to the activity of profiteers.

The next illustration presents a note, printed in orange tint, which possibly may seem out of place in the present article. It is apparently French and might be considered more suitable for the

MORE ENEMY WAR CURRENCY. 29

OBVERSE

REVERSE

article in the May issue, in which French emergency money was described. The note, however, is of German origin, for it was issued in territory *occupied by the enemy*, and the circular purple stamp, on the left of the obverse, has doubtless been styled by the exasperated and vivacious natives of the district as " la marque de la bête." Truly certain rivers of France have acquired immortal fame in this awful but victorious struggle. Amongst them are numbered the Somme, the Marne, and the Aisne, on the banks of the last of which this note was current.

There is a strain of simplicity in the German which sometimes produces strange results. It is exemplified in this note of Füssen, portraying the struggle of the German Michael against a fearsome dragon, and the measure of success attained. The dismembered heads

typify Russia, Servia, Montenegro and Roumania; the three still upreared represent Britain, France and the United States awaiting the skilful attention of the Saint. Observe that, despite the mediæval mansion in the background, the artist has considered no shining armour but the loin cloth of a barbarian to be the garb most suitable for his hero. It is not for us to quarrel with his selection.

The later notes circulated by towns in the German Fatherland are of more artistic design than the extraordinary "ersatz" varieties, which were shown in the issue of this journal for December last (subsequently reproduced by permission in the Journal of the Canadian Banking Association published last April).

OBVERSE

REVERSE

Many of these newer specimens embody on their reverse ancient buildings of local interest which, happily for the inhabitants and for human decency, have escaped the fate meted out to many a glorious monument of mediævalism at Louvain, Ypres, Rheims and elsewhere. A fear haunted many lovers of old historical landmarks, more poignant than any sense of personal danger, lest a chance bomb, during the senseless raids upon London, might ruin for ever the ancient Abbey at Westminster, that wonderful epitome of all that is dear to the British race. The views of The Bridge of Bad Kreuznach and of the old town hall of Gorlitz are suggestive of other ancient relics, just as lovely and just as precious to dwellers in their vicinity, that have been utterly ruined or reduced to mere skeletons of their former splendour during the recent saturnalia of destruction.

It would be interesting to know whether the populace of Bad Kreuznach, which, as will be seen in the accompanying illustration, placed portraits of some of the chief militarists upon its notes, is still as heartily disposed to place these leaders in a place of honour.

One of the notes here shown was issued by the manufacturing town of Saarbrucken, just outside the borders of Alsace, ever memorable as the scene of the first engagement during the Franco-German War of 1870.

New designs have been employed recently for the Reichsbank notes. They are in strong contrast to the pre-war descriptions, suggesting wood-cuts rather than steel engravings, and appear to be unusually easy to counterfeit. In view of the vast number in existence this liability is likely to be a serious drawback.

SO CALLED TABORA GOLD SOVEREIGN

BRASS COIN FORMED FROM CARTRIDGE CASES

GERMAN EAST AFRICAN CURRENCY
SILVER
NICKEL
COPPER

D

The campaign in East Africa—the most creditable, on the score of military skill, of all those waged by the enemy, and where their redoubtable leader, Von Lettow, was able to contest a losing fight until the very day of the Armistice—gives the emergency currency issued by the German East African authorities an interest of its own. Foremost stands the so-called Tabora sovereign, which was nominally good for 15 rupees like the British anti-type, but contains only about four-fifths of its gold contents, being 750 instead of 916 parts in the thousand fine. It is a remarkable curiosity, and as such is now worth several times its nominal value. In recent times no Power, esteeming itself of the first rank, has struck and issued a *gold coin* defective as to its contents of precious metal. Mr. S. W. Beesley, in charge of the National Bank of India Branch

at Tanga, to whose courtesy the loan of the specimens here shown is due, wrote thus concerning them:—

"Gold produced from Sekengi during the war was coined into Rs. 15 pieces at the workshops of the Daresalaam Railway, and issued to the German residents of the better class. From one prisoner of war, I learnt that none were issued to those under the rank of sergeant, and two were issued to each married man having his wife in the colony. Report has it that only about 1,200 of these coins were struck, that they were partly intended as mementoes of the war, that they only contain about Rs. 10 worth of gold, and that an enterprising goldsmith in Zanzibar made them for export in 1917. The die for these gold coins was cut in Daresalaam by a Ceylonese goldsmith, who was seized by the Colonial Government and compelled to work under the strictest supervision.

"Subsidiary war coinage was also issued, the 20-heller piece being most common, while very occasionally a 5-heller piece was met.

Earlier coins were well struck from what appears a suitable medium, but later coins were said to be made of used cartridge cases and are stamped in a very slovenly manner."

A silver "Rupie" though evidently, by the date of issue, pre-war, figures amongst the illustrations. It has been included because of its probably unique style of design, viz., the head of the German Emperor, of arrogant mien, surmounted by a *military helmet*. This symbol, for such it is, is not borne upon the coins of any other Power laying claim to civilisation. It typifies the attitude of Germany toward subject races, and demonstrates the motive which has impelled the assembled Powers at Versailles to place their mandate in hands that base their title to authority upon

other grounds than force. The contrast between the position of the bearer of this head-dress in 1911 and in the present year cannot fail to strike the imagination. In this connection, the excellent taste displayed by cartoonists in this country, who have abandoned the fallen Emperor as the subject of their pencil, is worthy of note.

As a memento of the passing of German East Africa into the control of another Power, a plate showing a complete set of the pre-war metallic currency of this colony has been here shown. The three silver coins, rupie, ½-rupie, and ¼-rupie are silver, the 10 heller and 5 heller, perforated, are nickel, and the remainder, ½, 1 and 5 heller, are copper. The last mentioned is an unusually large and handsome coin. It is noteworthy that the word "heller," an old German and modern Austrian value, is used instead of "pfennig" inscribed upon the coins of the German Empire at home.

During the war, the Germans printed in the office of the "Deutsche Ost Afrika," Daresalaam, "interim" notes of the following denominations:—Rs. 1, Rs. 5, Rs. 10, Rs. 20, Rs. 50, Rs. 100, and Rs. 200. These notes were secured against Government lands, and were signed by a Treasury official, the Manager of the Deutsche Ost Afrika Bank, Daresalaam, and initialled by three other officials. Several kinds of paper were used in printing

them, either in order to mark different series, or for the prosaic but practical reason that stocks of paper were low and the printers had to use whatever they could get.

The varieties of paper employed are extraordinary, comprising packing descriptions of different thicknesses, canvas backed and otherwise. Amongst the colours are greys, greens, yellows, buffs and browns—in a bewildering number of shades. The three notes selected for reproduction are respectively white (one rupee), brown, and verdant green. What are the present value of these notes, and whether they will ever be redeemed remain open questions.

It is a sad result of the War that Germany, as a nation, should have debarred itself by militarism running riot from applying its valuable qualities of method, order and industry to the uplift of the African races, a task to which other European nations have been able to set their hands with a present measure of success, and some hope of greater things to come. The threefold reference in the German acceptance of the peace terms to the *honour* of that nation, implying as it does that *honour* does not consist in good faith, chivalry and regard for human life, so much as in avoidance

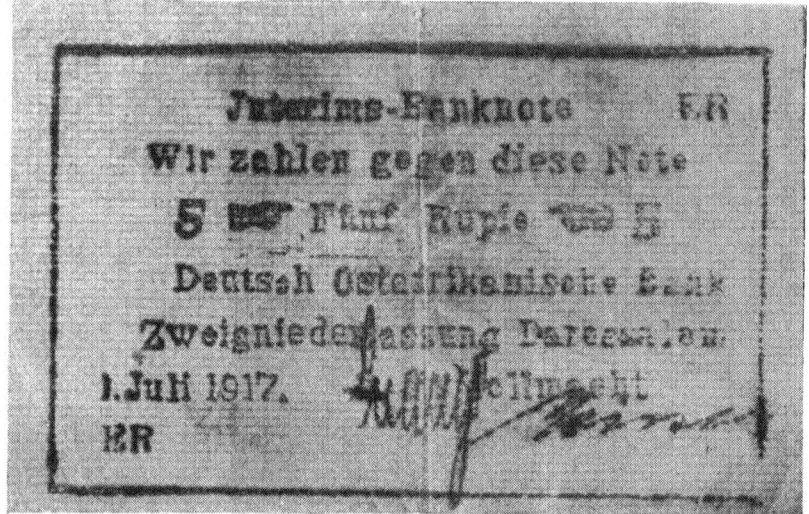

of just penalties for breaches of their observance, will remain a lasting memorial of moral obliquity. The fate of Germany is another indication of that clear insight into the springs of human destiny held by the One who said *all they that take the sword shall perish with the sword*. Blood and Tears are a poor foundation for a building intended to endure.

BELGIAN WAR COINS

CHAPTER IV.

BELGIAN WAR CURRENCY.

HE very mention of Belgium in connection with the War instantly recalls to mind the tall figure, with fearless eyes of blue, worthy inheritor of ancient chivalry, sans peur and sans reproche, for whom this country reserves a welcome exceptional in warmth and heartiness. Few bestowals of the Garter gave more pleasure to the British public than that to this Belgian King, for it emphasized the true Knighthood which was already his. Much as we admire the Belgian King, we must not however forget that it was the ready response to the call of duty on the part of the Belgian People themselves which enabled him to sustain the honour of the Nation over which he reigned. The writer will always remember the description of an eyewitness of that never to be forgotten and most fateful day in Belgian history, when King Albert rode home from the sitting of the Belgian Parliament, after its decision to uphold Belgian neutrality. Behind the King was a carriage bearing Queen Elizabeth, weeping unrestrainedly before the populace, with good cause indeed as she realised what it meant—a severance from her Bavarian kindred—one of whom was in command of forces advancing against her adopted country. Bravely and faithfully did she sustain the burden of a Crown!

The story of Belgium's war currency is also full of romance; it is instinct with that indomitable and stubborn pluck, of which Burgomaster Max has been so striking an exponent.

Between the 27th July and the 1st August, 1914, not less than fifty million francs of silver money were withdrawn from the Treasury in payment of notes; this amount, together with the pieces previously in circulation in Belgium, was promptly hoarded. The Belgian Government, however, with a foresight which is much to their credit, had already provided for the currency difficulties which were certain to attend a European War, by the following expedient. Eight million notes of five francs (previous to the war the lowest denomination of note was 20 francs), representing altogether

40,000,000 francs, had been printed and numbered in readiness ever since 1912. The notes needed only the imposition of a date and the signatures of the Governor and Treasurer of the Banque Nationale before being available for issue. Thanks to this admirable provision, the new notes were put into circulation the very day after the publication of the royal decree on August 2nd, 1914, authorising the issue. The necessity of thus forecasting events arose from the awkward geographical position in which Belgium is situated, as the result of which it was fated to become, not by any means for the first time, the cockpit of Europe.

The quickness of wit for which Belgians are renowned enabled them, in currency matters—as well as in other ways, such as the propagation of news—to circumvent the German invaders. When the enemy reached Brussels, money reserves and the plates for the striking of notes had already been conveyed to Antwerp; when Antwerp fell, these valuable articles were at the Bank of England, much to German annoyance and chagrin. The 5 franc notes printed in Antwerp had a rose-coloured instead of a red centre. The very fact of this transfer, however, prevented notes being issued in the quantities necessary to pay out readily the Bank deposits, etc., as required. The Banque Nationale thereupon issued a number of new notes to the value of 200,000,000 francs, entitled "Billet de Compte courant" (in notes of 1,000, 100, 20, 2 and 1 francs), which, however, soon failed to meet the demand.

The Germans then decided to deprive the Banque Nationale (still the official organ of the Belgian Government) of its privilege of issuing notes, and threatened to create Darlehenkassen or Loan banks (possessing power to issue notes on the security of property) similar to those instituted in Germany during the War. This

proposal by no means suited the Belgians, for it would have placed the country, so far as finance was concerned, absolutely under the thumb of Germany; in other words, it would have deprived the Belgians of all control over their own currency. Hence a suggestion was made (ultimately approved by the German authorities) that the Société Générale de Belgique should receive power to issue notes. This was done, notwithstanding that the enemy in occupation imposed certain onerous conditions. The German Government widely circulated a report that this action of the Société Générale

was impelled by its Pro-German proclivities. This Communiqué was an infamous lie, and should be nailed to the counter as such. The following extract from the official report of the Banque Nationale to the King after the Armistice clearly demonstrates the fact :—" It was in full agreement with the Banque Nationale that the Société

Générale assumed the task of issuing temporarily bank notes and that the methods of this issue were settled. We desire to put on record the disinterested attitude of the Société Générale de Belgique, which all through the most difficult negotiations had but one aim—to serve the country, and to preserve a central bank of issue which was indispensable to its economic life." The fact that this cordial co-operation between the two Banks naturally was concealed from the enemy authorities did not warrant the dissemination of the false statement that the Société Générale had played the traitor.

The Société Générale reproduced upon their franc note a portrait of the Orleans princess Louise Marie, who was the second wife of Leopold I. of Belguim, the wise and kind Uncle by marriage of Queen Victoria. His first wife, it will be remembered, was the daughter of our George IV., and the child of the marriage, had it lived (and its descendants, if any), would have reigned over the

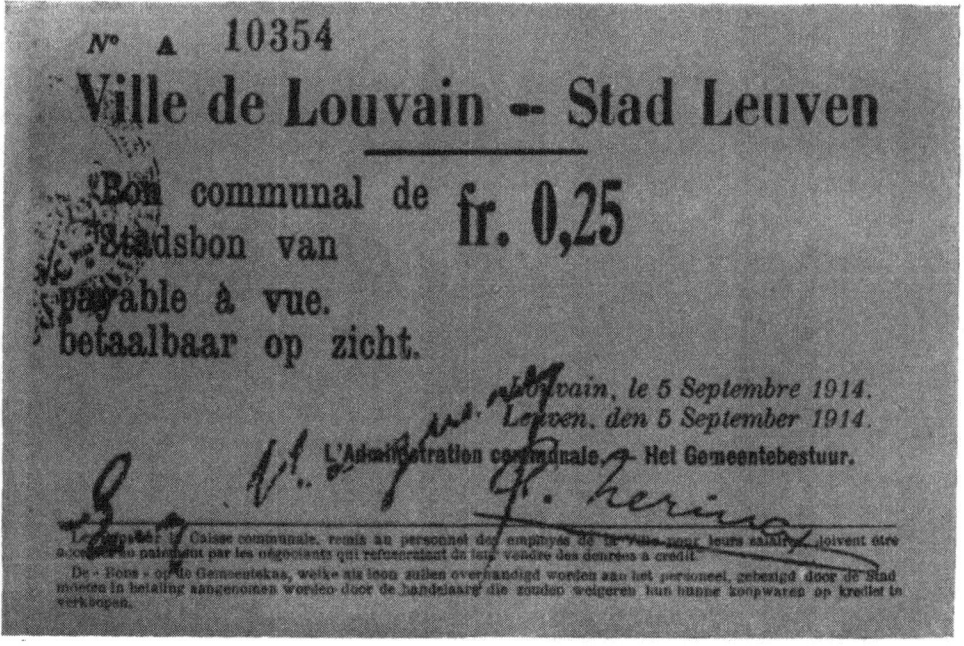

British Empire. Queen Louise Marie's expression is sad, and seems to be in keeping with the painful circumstances in which the note came into existence. It will be observed that the wording on one side of the note is in French, on the other in Flemish. In a similar fashion Belgian silver pieces are struck, half as francs and half as franks so as to conserve the amour propre of each race. As might be expected, the German authorities objected to the portrait of this lady being so much in evidence, and an imperative request was made that some other figure should be employed. As a result the fine head of Rubens, here reproduced upon a twenty franc note, was substituted for that of the Queen.

The early pieces of *local* paper money are of special interest, revealing as they do the destitute condition of the populace soon after the German occupation. The Belgian Red Cross reproduced three in a booklet sold for the benefit of its funds. The wants of the poor in Brussels were supplied by means of a set of three brown coupons—the first for clothing, the second for food, and the third for coal. Louvain paid the wages of its employés by coupons issued upon the town Treasury, of which a pink specimen for twenty-five centimes is here shown. Wilsele issued probably the

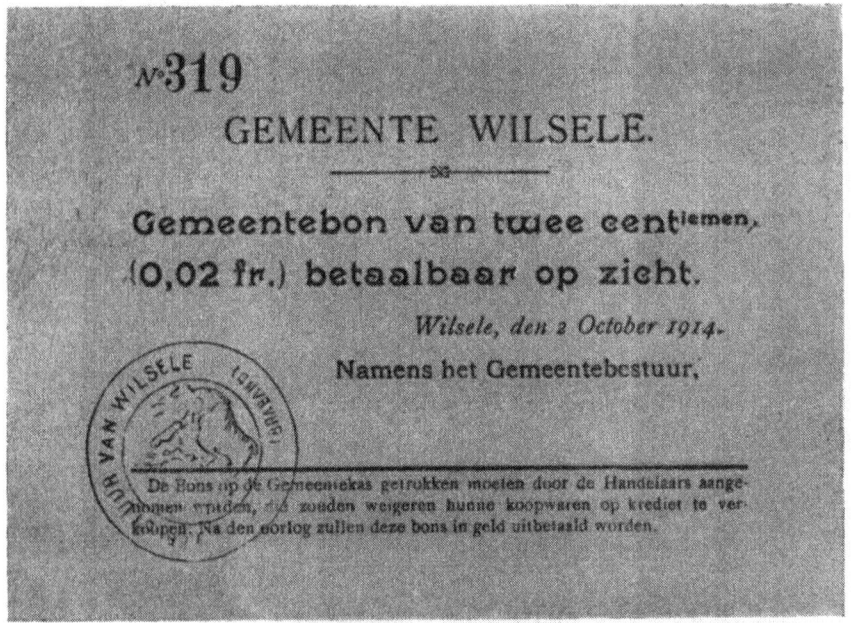

lowest denomination of paper money—namely two centimes—outside Russia where 1 Kopek notes have been circulated. This yellow document states that it is issued by the town Treasury and must be accepted by tradesmen who are not prepared to grant credit. After the war it is to be redeemed in cash.

A twenty-five centime cardboard note was issued by the Food and Health Committee of Alost, and was only available for the poor at the shops of the Committee. Bruges used a twenty-five centime note dated 1st June, 1915, showing the town arms upheld

48   BELGIAN WAR CURRENCY.

by a bear; while Ostend—the Mecca of many British tourists—issued a similar note in 1916, to be payable three months after the conclusion of peace.

In order to replace former coins of nickel—the material of which was so much in demand by the enemy for war purposes that they tore the very handles from chests and other furniture—5, 10, 25, and 50 centime pieces were struck in zinc. The name of Belgium, it

will be noticed, is inscribed in two languages, and the Belgian Lion is shown in a singularly pugnacious attitude, a symbol amply justified by events.

A RUBENS NOTE

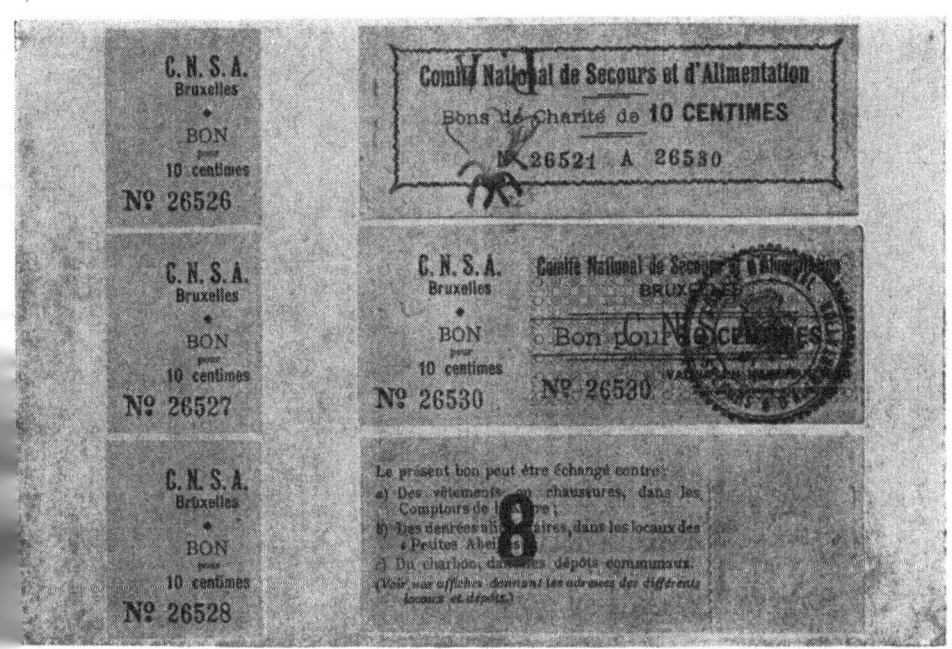

MONEY FOR BRUSSELS POOR

BELGIAN WAR CURRENCY.

Local coins were also struck. Ghent produced a *brass* five franc piece of really noble appearance, and also subsidiary pieces in the same metal of an unusual shape--square with rounded corners. It also put out ten centime pieces of thick millboard, of which the pattern is highly artistic in dull green and yellow. Dottignies printed a twenty-five centime note in blue upon somewhat flimsy material. The ten centime circlet of Mouscou is white upon a chocolate card, and the twenty-five centime oblong note of Quievain is black upon a dark brick coloured ground; whilst the ten centime note of the Commune of Rouveroy is printed upon a lighter shade of the same material. The town of Binche issued a business like specimen printed on light pink cardboard with surcharges of value and signatures in bright vermilion.

A very serious currency problem eventually arose owing to the circulation of a large number of German Marks, for which the German authorities imposed upon the populace an exchange value of 1·25 francs per mark. The number of these mark notes increased greatly, owing to the quantity introduced by the troops in occupation and by the forcible acquisition on the part of the German authorities of goods, agricultural produce, etc. Belgium was justly renowned for its live stock of kine; these naturally were not overlooked by the unwelcome visitors. When the accumulation acquired disquieting proportions, as viewed both from the standpoint of exchange and the increased fiduciary circulation of the Reichsbank, the German authorities sought to concentrate the marks in the Banque Nationale and in the issue departments, in order to demand their forcible repatriation by means of payments into special accounts current opened with German Banks, against which notes were to be issued by the Société Générale. This effort was violently resisted until the permission of the Belgian Government at Havre was obtained on condition that the eventual repayment of these marks should be at the exchange of 1·25 francs per mark. As the German authorities refused to recognise the intervention of the Belgian Government, a deadlock resulted. Finally the German Government delivered an "ultimatum," non-compliance with which would have involved the sequestration of the resources of the Banque Nationale and of the Société Générale, that is to say, unless a transfer to Germany of the marks in question was authorised

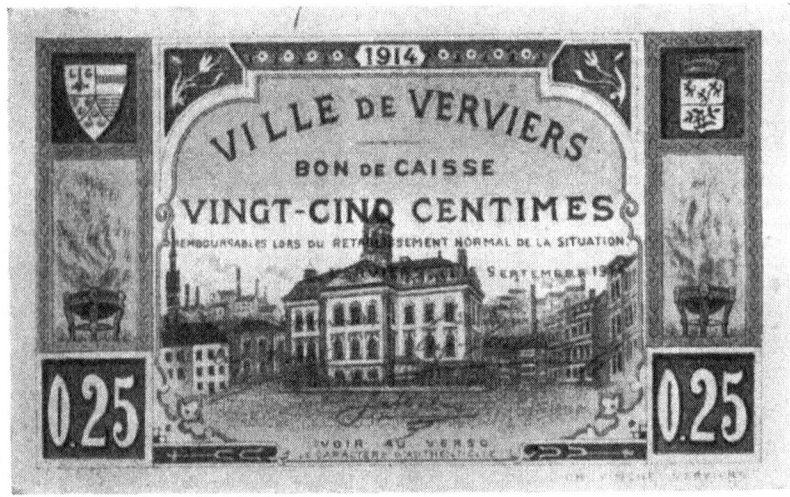

within 24 hours. As the Société Générale remarked in its 1918 Report, "this was requisition by force, the threat of the burglar."

This gallant conduct on the part of banking officials in defence of the financial interests of the Belgian people was not unaccompanied with serious danger to their lives and liberty. Monsieur Carlier, the Director of the Banque Nationale, was arrested as he stepped out of the train at Antwerp, and was deported on the 31st July, 1916, to Germany, where he was detained without trial until the Armistice was signed.

During part of the occupation certain towns and villages issued local paper money—notably Verviers, a manufacturing centre about 14 miles from Liège of glorious memory; the main part of the design is brown, with a view of the town in bright green. A set of these issued by Malines—famous for its mechlin lace—is here presented. They are a reminder of the giver—Dr. E. Hamel—

the dignified chief of its Athénée, who, after undergoing, with his wife and eight young children, the perils of bombardment, escaped, with but the clothes they wore, to find a temporary asylum in this

country. At the call of his Government, he left his family, returned to face the dangers of his occupied fatherland, and resumed his duties, but, unable to comply patriotically with enemy orders, was deprived of his position and exiled to a country district. It is satisfactory to know that his pro-German successor was promptly imprisoned as soon as the Germans evacuated the district.

Some of the names recorded on these notes, such as those of Tienen (Tirlemont) and Leuven (Louvain) recall painful episodes

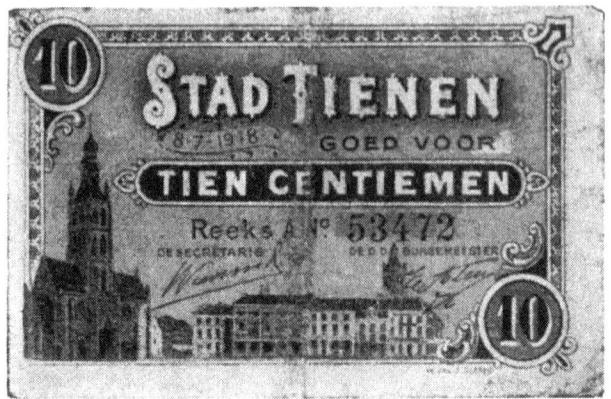

during the campaign of frightfulness, perpetrated with a view to cow the Belgian spirit. On the note circulated by the last named is a view of the renowned town hall, the only ancient building of any importance left standing in this fine old town after the destruction brought by the Hunnish hordes. How else can invaders be described, who spared neither sex in murder, nor antiquity in

pillage and rapine? The note is printed in fiery red, fit reminder indeed of the flames which destroyed the priceless treasures of the ancient university and library of this Flemish City! It is difficult to write with restraint when tokens like these revive memories of such vile atrocities, and the task is rendered none the easier by the cool assumption of the German race to be apostles of the highest culture.

The note issued by the town Aalst (Alost) is especially artistic; in contrast to those of d'Ath and Vezon, Elene and some other places, where they resemble train tickets or passes for the theatre. The ten centime note of Soignies is even perforated at the edge

Simple and trivial though they be, we almost shrink from speculating as to the vicissitudes through which they may have passed before they reached the engraver's hands in order to figure in these pages.

Was one retrieved from the body of some poor peasant forced at the point of the bayonet to act as living screen to an advancing German column, or was it a silent eyewitness of one of these outbreaks of brutal lust, which have desecrated so many Flemish homes, and covered the German name with lasting infamy?

These bits of paper have served their day and generation. They have been, each to some degree, a weapon to withstand the attack of the Evil Thing which menaced the liberties of Europe, and of civilization at large. It is difficult for anyone—staid Banker though he be—to view these pitiful evidences of the war, reminders of the

dire extremity of martyred Belgium, without a throb of emotion and a deep sense of gratitude to the Almighty, that the heart of that sorely pressed country beat true to its noblest impulses in the day of her fierce trial.

ROSTOFF s/DON NOTE

CHAPTER V.

RUSSIAN WAR CURRENCY.

E are too near the dread events of the past five years to gain their true perspective. *We* are history and therefore we ourselves form an integral part of the scene. Our emotions have been so stirred that we lack power to take a calm and detached survey, hence minor features often assume undue importance in our eyes. Of one great outstanding fact, however, we are conscious, the figure who had usurped the centre of the world's stage made a gigantic effort, when face to face with ruin, to emulate in his blind rage the last exploit of Samson. He sought to involve the whole of Europe in one common doom by wrecking two Empires which like two pillars formed its main support. One fell, but the other, thank God! stood firm.

Who would have imagined that the colossal power whose policy often has been a nightmare to the Indian Government, whose peoples, renowned for their blind loyalty, outnumbered those of the United Kingdom by three to one, would collapse like a building formed of cards! As the panorama recedes from our vision the stupendous catastrophe presented by the Russian Revolution will be the more appalling as we realise to the full its immensity and the widespread misery which it left in its train.

Bad finance, like ill-tempered mortar, made the disaster the more easy of accomplishment. Quite early in the war paper currency in denominations of so small size as to constitute a record was put into circulation by the Russian Government. They consisted of one, two, three and five kopeks, printed respectively upon a background of yellow, purple, green and blue. The one kopek note was one hundredth part of a rouble, nominally 25 pence—so that the note at this sterling value would have been worth one farthing. The value of the rouble, however, was only worth at the time of issue about half that price, and before the Imperial régime came to a close had fallen so low that the value of the kopek was only

equal to one-sixteenth of a penny. This series of notes is remarkably well executed. Design, engraving and paper are all excellent; the paper even bears a watermark. So good is the manufacture that in the case of the lowest denomination the cost of production must in all probability have exceeded the nominal value.

The great scarcity of small change after the outbreak of war caused postage stamps to perform in several countries the temporary function of currency, but it was only in Russia (and in Madagascar) that the authorities were ingenious enough to adapt postage stamp designs specially for the purpose. Three of the designs for stamps —namely, those for 10 (blue), 15 (dull red) and 20 (olive) kopeks— were printed upon specially thick paper and inscribed upon the back to the effect that the respective documents were to have the same legal currency as silver coin of similar value. It will be observed that the edge was perforated, so that the notes could be issued in sheets like stamps. The designs belong to what was called the Romanoff issue of postage stamps, each of which bears the portrait of a Russian Sovereign; these three bear respectively those of the Czars Nicolas II., Nicholas I. and Alexander I.

Of the lower values three, namely, the one, two and three kopeks, are also reproduced. These differ somewhat as to the inscription upon the reverse; in these specimens the number of kopeks is inserted for which each was intended to act as money. The Czars represented are respectively Peter I., Alexander II. and Alexander III. The ill fate which pursued the rulers of Russia is shown by the fact that out of the six Czars portrayed upon these notes, three of them, Peter I., Alexander II. and Nicholas II. met with violent deaths at the hands of their subjects. The destruction of the last mentioned, at the same time and place as his entire family, comprising wife, three daughters and youthful heir, is the most awful tragedy that has befallen the Russian Royal House—unlucky though it has ever been—and possibly exceeds in horror that experienced by any other Royal Family in recent times.

The German authorities, in accordance with their usual practice with regard to invaded territory, imposed an issue of their own creation upon the unhappy inhabitants. After denuding them of any precious metal upon which they could lay their hands, they introduced money struck in iron, ample supplies of which were at their disposal. A specimen is here shown.

RUSSIAN WAR CURRENCY.

On the obverse the value is expressed in Russian, impaled upon the design with which the world, and the German people themselves, have been regaled *ad nauseam*—the *Iron Cross*. The reverse bears German words to this effect: " Territory of the Commander in Chief in the East."

As soon as the Germans made good their grip upon Russian Poland they instituted loan banks—Darlehenkassen (on similar lines to those instituted in their own country) in order to create credit and incidentally to force notes issued by these banks upon the

unfortunate inhabitants in payment for military and other supplies. The security behind these notes must now be of a most dubious character. Both the notes here illustrated are dated Posen, April 17, 1916, and bear three signatures, Michalowski, Hamburger and Kauffmann—two of the three, it will be observed, are German names. The notes are of an extraordinary multi-lingual character, and may serve, should the world last long enough for the languages to become extinct, to interpret them for future ages, like the Rosetta stone! The face of the note is printed in German, but the inscription upon the back is in no less than three local languages, Polish,

LOAN BANK NOTE

RUSSIAN ARCHANGEL

etc. The German phrase upon the face reads thus:—"Whoever imitates, falsifies or puts such notes into circulation will be punished with imprisonment up to eight years." A threat which, like many others, the utterer has lost the power to enforce.

It has been asserted that the German authorities forged Imperial Russian notes in enormous quantities. Whether this be true or not, the Germans have themselves to thank for such reports. Their known methods of dealing with helpless foes have been so mean and despicable that rumour considers no expedient too base for them to perpetrate.

Once, however, that the downward path of note inflation began to be trod in Russia, it needed a literary Hogarth to picture adequately the road to ruin. The Russian Imperial Government financed the war mainly with paper money, the succeeding Kerensky régime adopted the same simple but dangerous plan with notes of its own design, whilst the Bolshevik Government went one better, or rather one worse, by printing at the utmost speed notes of the Imperial as well as the Kerensky pattern, indiscriminately. The combined output was stated in February, 1919, to have reached £30,000,000 a day in nominal value, and the grand total outstanding on January 31, 1919, is put at the almost incredible figure of 180,000,000,000 roubles. In May, 1918, it was stated that the Russian Government had fixed the ratio between the paper and the gold rouble at 1 to 25, that is to say, placing the notes at an official discount of 96 per cent. The Soviet money actually bears as authority the signature of a convicted forger. A commission endowed with special powers for the investigation of the activity of the Bolsheviks in Siberia and the Far East, says the Russian Liberation Committee, has published a series of data obtained by judicial investigation of the rule of the "Soviet Power" in Blagovestchensk, on the Amur. The Chief Commissary of the Amur, Krasnoshchokoff (whose name appeared on the paper money issued by the Soviets), was a convicted forger; Moukhin, the President of the Blagovestchensk Soviet, had also been condemned to penal servitude for forging bank notes, his deputy, Shatkovsky, was an exile, a former robber; his assistant, Hakiloff, was a convicted robber. The Food Commissary, Suikin, was a convict, sentenced for arson; the Commissary of Education, Korovin, a convict sentenced for murder. The Commissary of Police, Mitin, was an exile who had served a term of penal servitude, and his assistant, Philoppoff, was a convicted murderer, whilst the Commissary of Finance, Tilik, was a convict sentenced for participation in the robberies and incendiarism during the agrarian disturbances in 1906.

A strictly limited quantity of rouble notes, placed upon a gold footing by arrangement with the British Government, were issued in connection with the Expeditionary Force at Archangel; they are payable at Messrs. Barclays Bank at the rate of sixpence a rouble. The rouble note is printed in blue upon yellow. The effrontery of the Bolshevik authorities has been evidenced by the statement—

VLADIVOSTOCK

particularly brazen in view of the one hundred and eighty thousand millions of rouble notes in existence, for most of which they were responsible—that England was actively engaged in flooding Russia with *forged* notes.

The latest Kerensky designs for 20 and 40 rouble notes are unnumbered, and so rudimental in their simplicity, that they are more like luggage labels than documents of value.

The varieties of Russian notes are bewildering—comprising Transcaucasian, Ukraine and native Archangel notes. The last mentioned notes bear the statement that they are registered at the

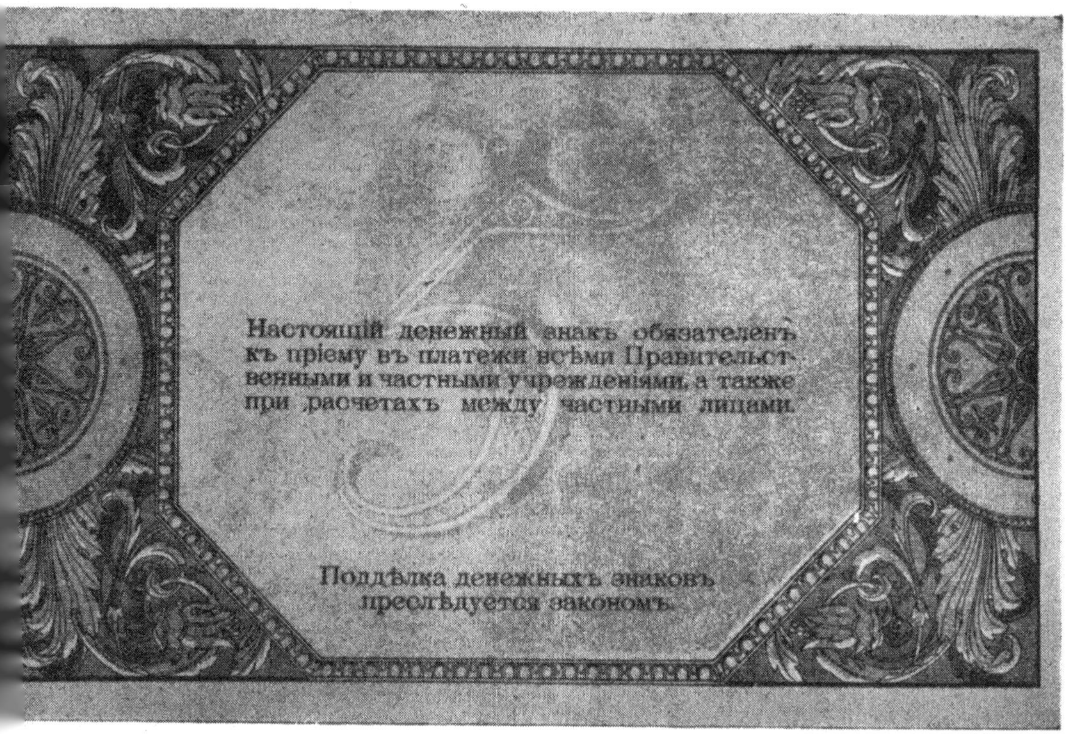

ROSTOFF s/DON NOTE

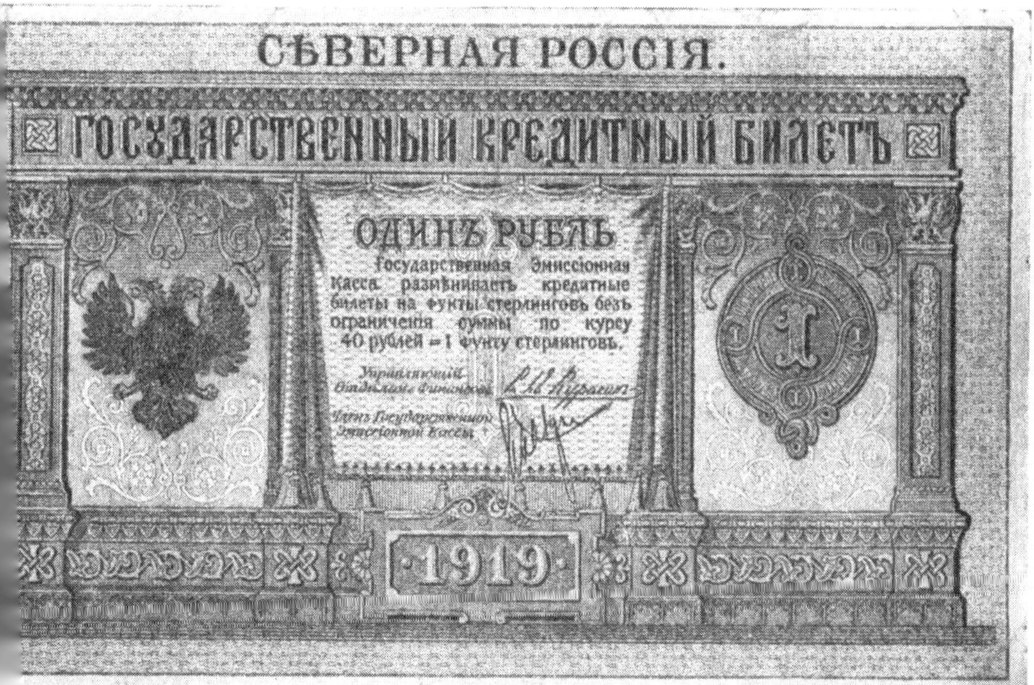

BRITISH ARCHANGEL

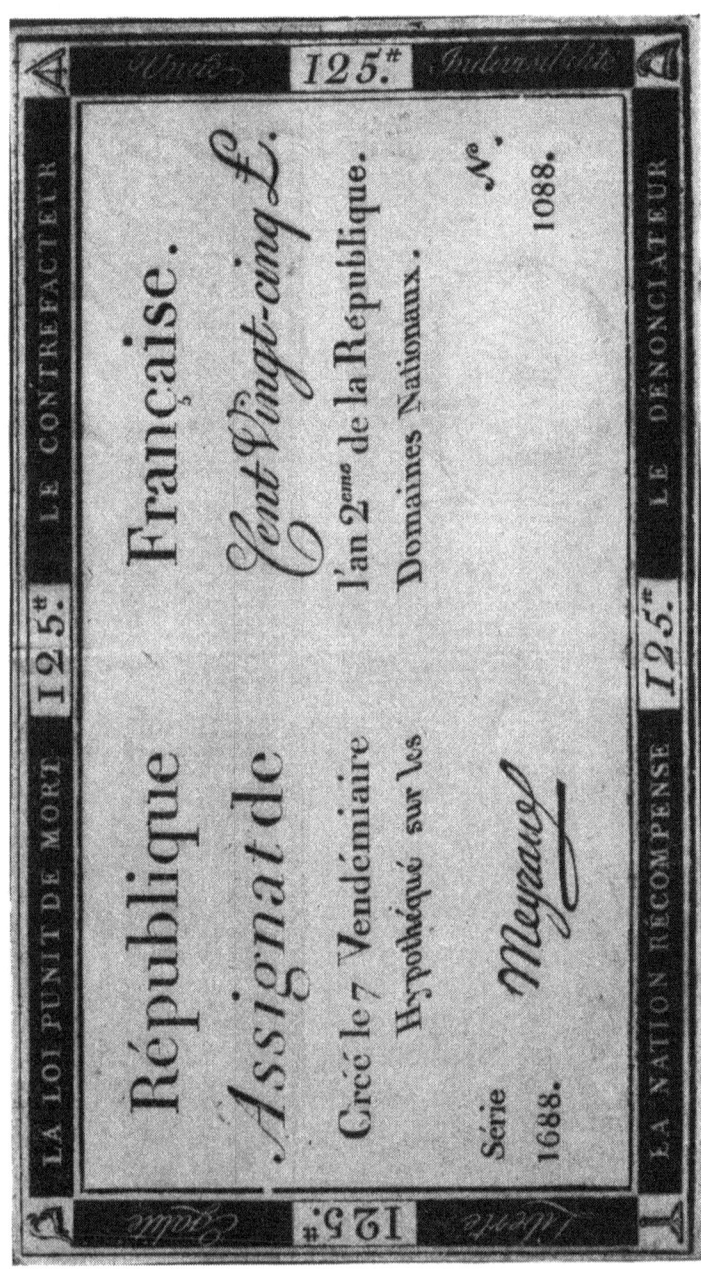

FRENCH ASSIGNAT

local branch of the State Bank. A series issued by the Rostoff s/Don Branch of the Banque de l'Etat are of more artistic design than most of the obviously emergency issues—they consist of the following denominations : 100, 25, 10, 5 and 3 roubles—the respective colourings are faint, but not unpleasing.

In addition to these issues on behalf of Governments there are notes circulated by local authorities, such as towns, amongst which figures Odessa.

Not the least of the problems which await Russia when it again enjoys the blessings of an ordered Government will be the regulation and systematic reduction of the mass of paper currency which has compelled trade in many districts to revert to a system of barter. Indeed, it is said that parcels of notes have changed hands by the thickness of the bundle, or even by their weight instead of their nominal value.

It has recently been asserted in the *Times* that the relation between the price of commodities necessary to sustain human life in Petrograd and currency has reached such an awful degree that a pound of bread commands 35 roubles, of potatoes 67, of butter 1,800, of horseflesh 500, of flesh unspecified (believed to be human) 100, of chicory 480, a gramme of saccharine 17, one herring 80, one apple 60, and that tea, coffee, sugar and clothes are practically unobtainable.

There is but one parallel to the epidemic of paper currency in Russia during the last five years, and that is the output during the French Revolution, but even that, enormous though it was, never approached such tremendous figures. The effect in each case has been the same, the notes became almost of nominal value. It is really surprising that the Russian notes, notwithstanding the far greater value put into circulation, have not yet become practically valueless, as did the French assignats.

This paper money was first issued by the French Government in September, 1790. By January, 1793, when war broke out between France and the United Kingdom, they had fallen to half their nominal value—when the Reign of Terror commenced in August, 1794, they were only worth 22 per cent. In June, 1796, the then total issue of thirteen thousand million francs were only equal to four hundred and forty millions in bullion value; before that year

ROSTOFF s/DON NOTE

ROSTOFF s/DON NOTE

was ended the value shrank to a mere fraction of one per cent. So that, assuming a loaf in the famine-stricken land was worth a franc in metal money, the miserable poor folk in those terrible days must have had to pay as much as 125 francs in assignats—the exact value of the specimen note here shown—for a few hours' supply of the staff of life. Almost valueless as this instrument of money was during its existence, there are few designs of paper money which excel its chaste and classical beauty.

The following extract from Messrs. Samuel Montagu & Co.'s Exchange Circular indicates the extraordinary relative value of paper money now current in Russia under the rule of the Soviet Government:—

"Bolshevik newspapers complain that the Soviet paper money issued after 1st June last is accepted unwillingly and at a heavy discount, which will hamper Finance Commissary Krestnisky in executing that part of the law which enjoins withdrawal of earlier notes and the substitution of Soviet notes. The Soviet issue is having the effect of pushing better money out of circulation. Even the despised Kerensky so-called 'Beer Labels' are relatively valuable. There are now four kinds of Central Government notes. The *Vozrozhdenie* publishes quotations in Minsk:—

100 Czar Roubles	640/50	Kerensky.
,, ,, ,,	310/315	Duma.
,, Duma ,,	200/205	Kerensky.
,, Kerensky Roubles	125/130	Soviet.

"These figures refer to the *design*, not to the *issuing Government*, as Czar roubles have been issued by all Governments, the Duma, and the Kerensky by both provisional Governments of 1917 and by the Soviet. At present a great flood of Kerensky notes flows into Soviet Russia from Warsaw and Vilna, thus increasing the discount. M. Vasiloff, a Moscow financial writer, estimates that three-quarters of the Czar roubles 'in circulation' are in reality hoarded."

We must be careful not to attach undue importance to the present condition of Russia, desperate though it appears to be, for the resources of the country are enormous and remain comparatively untouched. Its external debt is relatively small, whilst it contains a laborious population, together with magnificent forests and vast stretches of fertile soil only waiting to be turned into material wealth.

Given the *man* or *men* for whom all her well-wishers pray, the dire distress of Russia may be but a passing phase in the history of this great nation.

The sympathies of the world undoubtedly go out toward the educated classes in Russia, fiercely overborne by the proletariat which has barely emerged from a condition of serfdom akin to that

REVERSE KERENSKY NOTE

OBVERSE KERENSKY NOTE

in France and England during the middle ages, and has been suddenly precipitated into a maelstrom of revolution.

The geographical position of Russia, shut off from ready access to the sea, the great civilizing medium of the human race, has so hindered the march of modern ideas that the working out of her destiny will be, it is to be feared, a costly and painful process.

CHAPTER VI.

ALLIED WAR EMERGENCY MONEY.

A LUCIFER match is one of the most insignificant of articles, but the results of striking it may be incalculable. The Sarajevo tragedy in 1914, much as it shocked the moral sense of Europe, seemed to most people as of no international importance whatever. To the wicked plotters against the peace and liberties of the World, however, it was a useful spark to light up a bonfire, but they did not dream that the conflagration would consume property and industry worth possibly a hundred thousand million pounds, and destroy lives by the sword, starvation and famine—probably if the news from Russia be correct—*already* not less than sixty million in number.

The little state of Servia lay helpless from the very outset. When the enemy powers had a moment to spare from the pressing affairs upon their Western Front "the Assyrian came down like a wolf on the fold" and swept the ill-fated land from end to end. Mind cannot picture adequately, and surely need not attempt to do so, the horrors undergone by the retreating Servian troops, faced by foes whose instructions were not merely to defeat, but to exterminate. Of the 40,000 Servian lads of tender years who took part in that awful retreat only 6,000 survived.

The use of Servian National money ceased almost at once, and Austrian kroner, now worth some 1,200 instead of 24 to the British pound sterling, their pre-war value, were circulated by the victors. When we remember that Germany deliberately sought to destroy the monetary system of France after the War of 1870, the utter disrepute into which the currency of the late enemy countries has fallen (a discount of 95 per cent. has been touched in the case of marks), surely we cannot fail to recognise that though the mills of God grind slowly, the operation is exceeding sure.

In 1916, however, the National Bank of Servia was authorised to issue notes. A specimen, good for five dinars, printed in a dull blue, is here illustrated—the blank space is occupied by a watermark of a helmeted warrior, similar to that engraved on the other side. If the note be held up to the light it is visible on both the obverse and reverse.

One very interesting fact has come to light in connection with our Italian Ally. It is that the agreement which brought Germany, Austria and Italy into the Triple Alliance contained an express stipulation that Italy should be free from taking up arms against Great Britain. This proviso was dictated by a sentiment of gratitude for the sympathetic interest shown by Great Britain in the birth of Italian Independence and does that gallant nation honour. In any event, lovers of liberty, like the free Italian people, could have had little in common with the ambitions of their erstwhile allies.

The usual reason—shortage of subsidiary coinage—speedily led to the issue of one and two lire notes, the designs of which hardly do justice to the great artistic heritage of Italy. Strangely enough really fine specimens of notes were issued later on for use in Italian territory, but, alas! by enemy authority for the service of districts overrun by the hostile troops.

Possessing the advantage of interior lines, the Central Powers were able to launch attacks with the utmost swiftness and with overwhelming strength, at far distant points of the encircling front of the Allies. Belgium, France, Russia and Italy each in turn had to bear the brunt of these rude hammer blows, and to yield territory, first to be ravaged, and then to be administered by the merciless invaders in their own interests.

Two wide and rich provinces of Italy fell thus under Austrian domination, the Udine and the Venetian plain. The notes issued by the Commune of Udine are poor in execution and possess no striking feature, except a fine representation of a mediæval castle, doubtless the pride of the folk who lived around it. The colours are orange for the five lire and fifty centesimi, and dark blue for the one lire note.

Most people of cultivated taste watched anxiously the advance of the enemy toward Venice, that wonderful survival of a glorious past, the very stones of which have been full of charm to all who delight in the artistic and the beautiful. Day by day, enemy aircraft, from their base so dangerously close at hand, swept the sky above the island city, and rained incessant bombs, happily productive of more alarm and discomfort than of real damage.

The notes for five, ten and fifty centesimi, circulated by enemy authority in the occupied Venetian mainland, resemble mere coupons, printed respectively in blue, yellow and rose, but the higher denominations are really fine productions, of original and striking appearance. In every case the letterpress is inserted in a massive frame design, with colouring heavy and rich. Each bears on the obverse a finely

engraved female head, set in a medallion. So impressive is the general effect that the notes suggest the idea that the artist responsible for the design must have derived his inspirations from the genius of the locality, so rich in artistic treasure.

Though only three specimens are here represented the denominations of the higher valued notes rose to a very large figure. The one lire is printed in deep rose red, upon a ground covered with mauve lines, and suffused with a lighter shade of rose. The two lire is olive upon a ground of tawny yellow, with the medallion in lighter green. The ten lire is an indigo blue, with dull yellow background and has quite a noble appearance.

The notes of the next Ally to be mentioned have a special interest for the British nation. Queen Marie of Roumania is the granddaughter of our Queen Victoria, and, during the sad reverses which the Roumanian nation had to undergo, bore herself with unflinching courage and a fortitude not unbefitting the high lineage from which she sprang.

Soon after the outbreak of the Great War, Roumania, like other of the then neutrals, had to amplify its stock of currency by issuing paper notes of low denomination. The one leu and two lei issued by the Roumanian National Bank are printed in blue and mauve upon white paper; the designs are rather elaborate, and comprise female figures of somewhat anxious mien, suggestive of the difficult circumstances in which the nation was placed. The one leu shows Romulus and Remus mothered by the wolf. The five lei is extremely pleasing in colour—faint lake upon mauve. The two blank spaces display,

when the note is held to the light, antique male heads of differing designs. No black and white reproduction can give the charm of the reverse, which portrays, in various tints of the colours mentioned, a dainty maiden, plucking fruit from a tree, attended by her nude young brother. The two youthful figures are represented in very graceful attitudes.

In 1917 the Roumanian Minister of Finance made an issue of notes for ten, twenty-five and fifty bani. The designs are not unlike those usually placed on postage stamps; the King's bust is on the obverse and his arms on the reverse. The ten bani is green on olive, the twenty-five bani brown on yellow, and the fifty bani blue on brick-red.

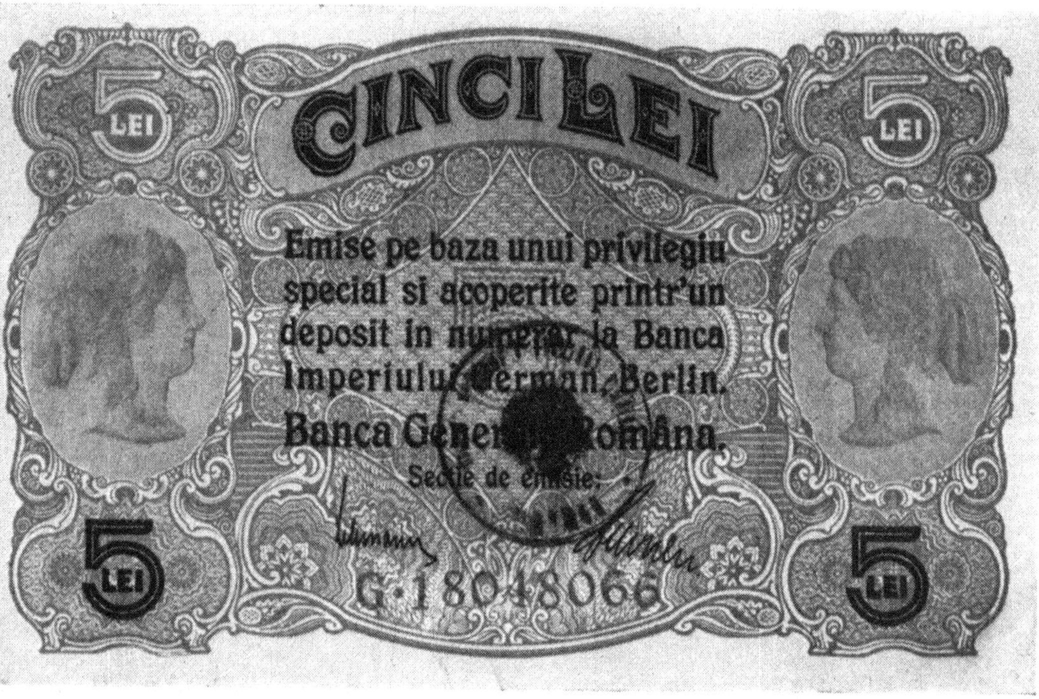
CINCI LEI
5 LEI
Emise pe baza unui privilegiu
special si acoperite printr'un
deposit in numerar la Banca
Berlin.
Banca
Româna.
Sectie de emisie:
G·18048066

5 LEI

G

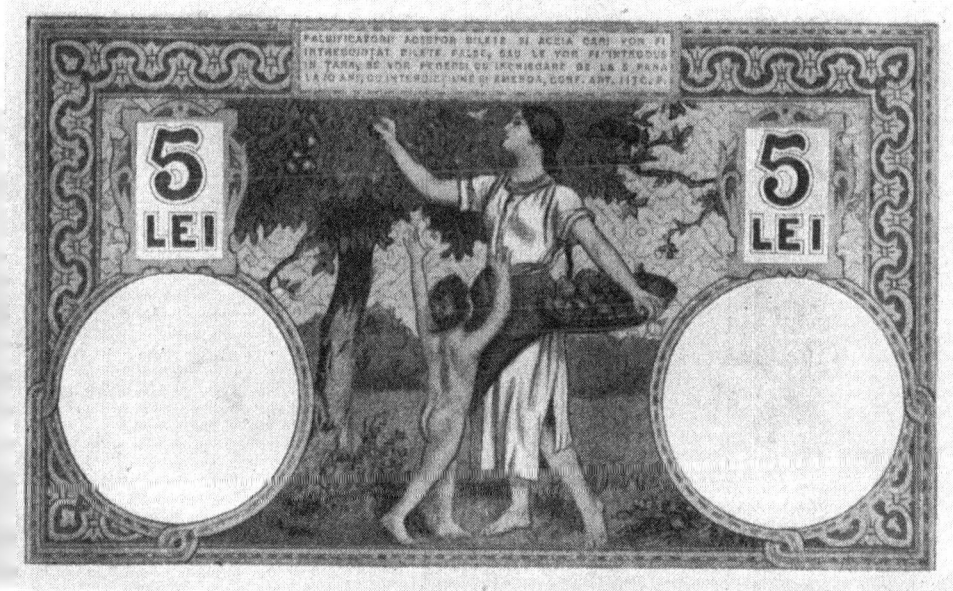

When, like other nations forming the ring round the Central Powers at bay, Roumania was forced to give way before a concentrated attack, and its territory was temporarily occupied by the enemy, a fresh series of notes were issued by the Banca Generala Romana. Each note bears the ominous words :—" Issued on the basis of a special privilege for those numbers registered and cash deposited with the Imperial Bank of Germany, Berlin." We have heard of cash deposited in a similar way by other unfortunate nationalities that had a like fate.

The country was flooded with these notes, and only those registered before a specified date with the Banca Generala Romana —a German institution—possessed any legal recognition. The one

always certain step taken by the ringleader of the gang was to loot the gold of friends and enemies alike, and to take the plunder to Berlin, by the same act adding to German resources, and ensuring the complete financial dependence of the helpless folk they enthralled. The twenty-five bani is ochre brown, the fifty blue, the one leu green and two lei red, and the five lei mauve.

Immense quantities of Austrian kronen notes were forced into circulation during the enemy occupation. A resolute effort is being made to redeem these in order to purify the currency. The quantity is estimated at four milliards of kronen, and the exchange is being made at the rate of two stamped kronen for one leu. The notes of the Banca Generala will also be replaced by notes of the National Bank.

In the course of describing the designs of emergency notes in this and preceding articles, attention has been drawn to the pleasing appearance which some of the specimens present. The crown of success, however, certainly rests on those of Greece, both on account of the beauty of design and the delicacy of colouring. The engraving

is of so elaborate a character that forgery seems to be almost impossible. The glorious sculptures of Ancient Greece are reproduced upon these notes in effective fashion. It is a matter for national pride that these exquisite little specimens were manufactured in the United Kingdom. The people of the British Empire, appreciative of the difficult position in which the Greek nation was placed, rejoiced that those external

influences which impelled them toward action unworthy of their ideals were resisted successfully, and that Greece ultimately ranged itself alongside the Allies in the fight for freedom. Fortunately for the reputation of Royalty, the fine impulse of *noblesse oblige* has impelled a King to identify himself usually with his adopted country, however painful the decision may have been. So much the greater is the odium that attaches to a Sovereign who fails to love his honour more than the ties of family.

It is a far cry to the Far East, but by no means beyond the scope of the Great War. The valuable services of the Japanese Imperial Navy in coping with raiders and submarines must not be forgotten. We reproduce here the distinctive notes of Japan, issued with the object of minimising the use of silver for coinage. The ten sen has a yellow, the twenty a green, and the fifty a pink background, and each is imprinted with a stamp of vivid vermilion. It is stated that these emergency notes are to be withdrawn from circulation. It was plain

evidence of the solidarity of the Allied cause that Eastern nations like Japan and Siam should spring to arms and assist in chaining the disturbers of the World's peace.

The United States of America, whose welcome entry into the allied ranks, almost exhausted by the prolonged and arduous contest, imparted renewed life and vigour, fortunately had no occasion to create any new form of currency during the war.

Let us hope that the day may come when Germany, having proved by actions a change of heart, may again be received with the right hand of fellowship. The time, however, is not yet, for the World cannot quickly forget the course of events that led to the War, and the ghastly sum of misery brought in its train, the evidence of which will remain for many generations to come. The very notes reproduced in this article show how complete are the links in the chain.

The best proof of repentance would be willingness on the part of the German people to shoulder the burden of financial reparation imposed by the Allies, the aggregate of which is but a fraction of the immeasurable destruction wrought by their wanton attack upon their pacific neighbours. The terms are far less onerous than those which the arrogance of Germany in the hour of her apparent success had threatened to inflict upon the Allies. The holocaust of human life must ever remain an unpaid debt.

CHAPTER VII.

NEUTRAL WAR EMERGENCY MONEY.

HE great war has revealed in startling fashion how intimately the destinies of nations have become interwoven at this stage of the world's history. In days gone by countries formed infrequently what may be described as a ring within which two warring nations fought out their quarrel to a finish. The facilities, however, afforded by railways, steamships and telegraph wires have brought about a vast increase of international trade, which cannot adequately be transacted without international banking accommodation, the ramifications of which extend almost to the very confines of the earth. Hence it was not the financial systems of protagonists alone that trembled at the terriffic shock of that dread and fateful August Bank Holiday of 1914. There was not a banking house in Europe whose responsible chiefs did not consult together with the utmost gravity as they sought to disentangle the threads of their international liabilities. It is a wonderful testimony to the sanity of Governmental action and to the excellent foundations upon which most modern banks are reared, that no great financial institution, either amongst the central powers, the opposing allies, or the countries which stood neutral, collapsed at the outbreak of war.

Although finance, private and official, retained the elements of stability, currency systems received such rude blows that the consequences have been nothing less than amazing to those conversant with these matters. Countries which remained neutral have been by no means exempt from the necessity of remodelling their currency arrangements. Take coins for instance. Bronze, a constituent of which is copper, has been the material used almost invariably for tokens of the lowest value. Copper was needed for munitions. When thousands of shells sometimes were launched to cause a fatality perhaps to only one combatant, it is plain that the copper tribute to the God of War—the "old German God" in whom the junkers put their trust—must have been enormous. Cut off from imports overseas, Germany first ransacked occupied territories of their pots and pans, door-knockers and bells. Then the bronze money followed suit, and such a high premium for copper was obtainable that the bronze coins of adjoining countries speedily began to be drawn over the border. Not only copper, but nickel also was in keen request for the presentation of sacrifices to the modern Moloch. In these circumstances the Scandinavian nations found it difficult to retain bronze coinage within their territory, and each was compelled to adopt substitutes. Sweden, Denmark and Norway, though independent kingdoms, possess identical descriptions of currency. They took naturally similar methods to deal with the difficulty, and minted iron coins in the denominations of 5, 2 and 1 ore. Although the composition of the coins is the same, the appearance and touch are different owing to the varied treatment of the metal. The first desideratum obviously was to prevent, if possible, the tendency of iron to rust. The Swedish mint coated its coins with nickel. The Norwegian mint applied some preparation which gives the coins the appearance of being varnished, whilst the Danish issue seems protected by some external application which leaves a dull surface. Of course it remains to be seen whether in the course of time, wear, damp and acids cause the rusting quality of iron to assert itself. Meanwhile the coins are certainly attractive as to material and of pleasing design. All these three thrones are allied closely to our royal house. The Danish King is cousin, the Norwegian, brother-in-law, and the Crown Prince of Sweden, who has lately lost his charming consort, is cousin-in-law to our King George.

The increase in cost of commodities and wages, and the rising price of silver—led to the issue of 1 krone notes, but the design and size of the notes were diverse. Several attempts were made by Denmark to secure a satisfactory specimen. The first was doomed to disaster, because a dried cod, which once served as money, was represented on the back of the note as a heraldic sign for Iceland. The designer had forgotten, however, that a change had taken place in the Coat of Arms, and that the island is now represented by a bird—the Icelandic falk. After the notes had been put into circulation by the National Bank of Denmark, the Icelandic Government called the Danish Government's attention to the mistake,

which was regarded by Icelanders as an insult. As a consequence, the notes were withdrawn from circulation and have become rarities commanding a very substantial premium. The 1914 note here shown is black on a light chocolate ground, whilst the 1916 note is dull blue on grey.

The Norwegian note is a rather poor production—faint black print and ornament upon a greenish blue background, with a white margin. The numerals are in red.

The Swedish note is remarkable for more than one reason. The flourishes around the more important lettering give a quaint old world aspect to the black diffused design, printed upon a faint green background of wavy lines. Further, the note is probably unique in one respect, namely, that the black of the design seems to be printed right through the paper, for the back of the note is the *exact reverse of the front, and all the letters read backwards.*

The next neutral country whose currency will be considered is Switzerland, whose geographical position was a source of peculiar anxiety to its inhabitants. Not only was it placed between Germany and France as a wedge, the crossing of which was a constant temptation to both combatants, but it was also, owing to its racial divisions, exposed to the risk, happily not materialised, of internal dissension through undue acts of sympathy with neighbours of kindred extraction. Sturdy commonsense and robust patriotism saved the Swiss State from trouble of this sort, but not from the severe trials arising from its isolation from other non-combatant states and from the consequent difficulty of securing such imports as were desirable to its economic life. Although work in munitions and other special industries were a source of profit, the advantage was probably outweighed by the lack of tourists, the cost of maintaining a military force in case of untoward developments, and other expenses attaching to the observance of strict neutrality.

In order to remedy the shortage of bronze coin, brass pieces were issued for 5 and 10 centimes. This is remarkable in view of the fact that Switzerland, as Helvetia, formed part of the old Roman Empire, which employed this metal on a large scale for the purpose. It is possible that the slang expression, " Have you any brass about you ?" (harking back to the coinage of the Cæsars)

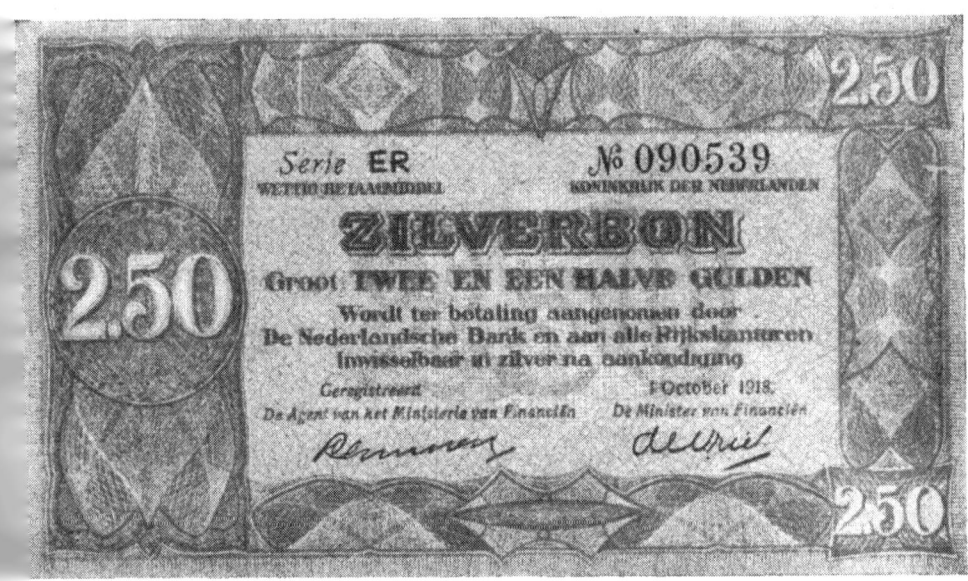

has been used by the Swiss youth in the last year or so with singular fitness.

The Swiss 5 franc note, dated August 1, 1914, is a fine production. It challenges comparison with the charming Greek notes, illustrated in the May number of this magazine. The designs are utterly unlike. There is a mechanical beauty about the Swiss note, one of colour and massive ornament, which is in absolute contrast to the delicate artistic finish of the Greek specimens. The colour scheme is in soft greens and browns, and it will be observed that the title of the National Bank is expressed in the three languages— German, Italian and French—which are spoken in the three groups of Cantons. The designer did well to conjure up a vision of William Tell in the left-hand medallion, for his heroic memory was a welcome inspiration in the anxious days of the encircling war.

Holland, too, had an extremely difficult and anxious part to play. She had no illusions as to what German success meant— German victory spelt Dutch enslavement. Her territorial position, however, rendered her comparatively helpless, *vis-à-vis* with so truculent a neighbour. It was as easy as possible for the province of Limburg instantly to be overrun, and effective resistance, short of submerging the larger part of the country, was impracticable. Further, for good or ill, she had to live alongside German territory, and the ties of future trade and a community of interest bred of propinquity, made her chary of giving offence.

She had opportunities of rendering great services as a neutral to both contending parties. The thousands of refugees from invaded Belgium and of combatants forced to take asylum, are not likely to forget the hospitable Dutch people.

Notes of small denominations had to be issued eventually owing to the difficulty of obtaining supplies of silver. Holland stands alone in recording the fact upon the notes themselves. It will be observed that they are styled zilverbons. The first issue of $2\frac{1}{2}$ guilders is plain, like the 1 guilder note, but the later issue of $2\frac{1}{2}$ guilders is more elaborate and not unlike the Swiss note to which reference has been made, but the colouring, a light blue on a yellow ground, creates a rather washed-out effect.

Poland cannot be described as a neutral, its unfortunate inhabitants having been impressed into the fray to fight against each

NEUTRAL WAR EMERGENCY MONEY. 95

other. Its notes, however, deserve a place in this series of articles, if only to record the reversal after many years of a grievous wrong. To attempt to stamp out nationality is an offence against the very soul of man, and we, who draw the breath of freedom, ever have sympathised with the Polish nation (to whose gifted sons we owe much artistic enjoyment), ever since its forcible division between two powerful neighbours.

Here are to be found illustrated half and one mark notes issued in Warsaw, the former printed in black on light green and the latter on yellow with a vermilion background to the eagle top panel. Each reverse bears coloured lines in rainbow fashion.

The Cracow note for half a korony is printed dark blue upon a background covered with light blue lines. The "$\frac{1}{2}$ korony $\frac{1}{2}$," the signatures and the eagle background are all in vermilion. This note possibly is also unique in one respect, for the obverse and reverse are exactly alike, except that on the reverse a number is substituted for the signatures.

It is to be hoped that the most friendly relations may be established with this restored sister to the nations of Europe, and that practical sympathy may be shown by the provision of material and such other help as she may need in order to enjoy an ordered and independent economic existence.

CHAPTER VIII.

BRITISH WAR EMERGENCY MONEY.

THE catalogue of the special money created during the clash of arms ends with a description of some of the varieties of paper currency which were issued for the first time during the stress of the Great War in the United Kingdom and Ireland and in other territory under the control of the British Crown, as well as in the Empire of India. Owing to Treasury Regulations it is not possible to reproduce British notes for illustration. They lie before the writer whilst he endeavours to picture them to the mind of the reader.

The Chief Cashier of the Bank of England was good enough to lend perfectly new specimens of the first two issues of Treasury currency notes, which, as they have practically passed out of circulation, merit careful description. Emphasis may well be made as to their improvised character. Neither in matters military, naval, nor financial can the country be said to have carried out the scout motto of " Be prepared." Our magnificent fleet had not even a haven of secure refuge when the gauntlet of defiance was flung before the country.

The first issue of currency notes for ten shillings and one pound were of small size. The specimen of the former measures $5\frac{1}{32}$ by $2\frac{9}{16}$ inches, whilst that of the latter is only $4\frac{15}{16}$ by $2\frac{1}{2}$ inches. As the £1 was intended to be larger than the 10/-, the specimen must have been a mutilated copy. The colouring is blood red for the ten shilling and black for the pound note. The paper, as used for British postage stamps, is of superior quality, watermarked with a number of G.R.'s, with crown superimposed. The pound note has between them three letters, S O, and a third letter, which is indecipherable, not unlike an S. Truly the notes were a financial S.O.S., but it is unlikely that the paper maker would have indulged his whimsical humour at such a serious time. Both notes are numbered in black—the ten shilling No. $\frac{A}{15}$ 240068 and the pound A 275987. The design of each is similar, and the engraving poor, but the pound note, that issued first, betrays the more hasty execution. On the left each bears a floral badge, with the letter G above and R below a medallion portrait of King George, surrounded by the inscription GEORGIUS V. D.G. BRITT. OMN. REX. F.D. IND. IMP. The centre is crossed by a bold ribbon, bearing the words "ten shillings" and "one pound" in white upon red and black respectively. On the right the ribbon bisects the indications of 10/- and £. Upon the base of the latter the clear written and now widely well-known signature of "John Bradbury" is appended diagonal fashion, with his official designation of "Secretary to the Treasury" placed horizontally.

The important information necessary to validate the notes is placed above the ribbon in Gothic character: "These notes are a legal tender for a payment of any amount. Issued by the Lords Commissioners of His Majesty's Treasury, under Authority of Act of Parliament." The reverses of the notes are plain.

The second issue of Treasury currency notes were of differing size. The ten shilling measures $5\frac{7}{16}$ by $3\frac{1}{32}$ inches, the pound $5\frac{7}{8}$ by $3\frac{3}{8}$ inches. The former note is again blood red, but not so deep in tone, the latter black. Both notes numbered in black respectively thus:— $\frac{M1}{86}$ No. 34177. $\frac{R}{4}$ No. 66216.

The paper is of excellent quality though very thin, and each note possesses a distinctive watermark of badges, etc., upon a wavy background. The former note bears "ten shillings" at the top, below are representations of a rose and a thistle, above a shamrock and daffodil (England, Scotland, Ireland and Wales), with 10/- on either side of the two bottom flowers. At each side of the note is shown G.R. with V inserted in the G and a crown superimposed. The watermark of the pound is identical, save that "one pound" and "£1" are substituted for "ten shillings" and "10/-."

Each description of note has on the left a medallion of King George, surrounded with a scroll carrying the same inscriptions as on the first issue, and surmounted with an imperial crown. On the right is a garter, also surmounted by the imperial crown, with the usual garter motto and medallion of St. George and the Dragon.

Words specifying the denomination are placed in the centre of each note upon a handsomely designed strap, and the value is again set out in figures on the left to balance the signature of "John Bradbury," written horizontally over his designation "Secretary to the Treasury."

A notable alteration is made in the wording, for at the top of these latter notes are the words "United Kingdom of Great Britain and Ireland." The remainder of the inscriptions runs: "Ten shillings" (one pound) "currency notes are legal tender for the payment of any amount. Issued by the Lords Commissioners of His

Majesty's Treasury, under the Authority of Act of Parliament (4 & 5 Geo. V. ch. 14)." The specification of the Act in brackets was not inserted upon the first issue.

An order was issued last year under the Currency and Bank Notes Act, 1914, calling in currency notes of the first and second issues. From June 11, 1920, these notes were to cease being legal tender, but could be presented for payment at any money order office in the United Kingdom, or at the Bank of England, or the Bank of Ireland, on any date before September 1, 1920.

The third and now widely circulating issue of Treasury notes needs no description.

The second issue of British Treasury currency notes was surcharged in Arabic character for use in Turkish territory under occupation. The surcharge on the ten shilling note was black, and red on the pound note, and the notes remained good tender in the United Kingdom and Ireland, though probably they found their way to the Bank of England almost as soon as they reached this country. The bold Arabic characters upon the ten shilling note indicate that it is valuable for 60 Turkish piastres; it was exchangeable in Egypt at anything between 45 and 48 piastres.

The Egyptian Government issued Government currency notes for 5 and 10 piastres (1s. and 2s.). The obverse of the five piastre note is printed in lilac upon a green background. A conventional lotus flower carries upon its blossom the P.T.S. on either side. At the foot is a view of a caravan wending a desert journey. The obverse bears an intricate machined pattern in blue with two large sphinxes facing each other at the bottom; both of these, for some unknown reason, have lost their noses.

Well wishers of Egypt—those who have seen its remarkable emergence under British tutelage from a state of desperate insolvence during the Ismail *régime*—will watch with interest the exercise of independence. Before the British occupation in 1882 the very date trees were taxed, and the ill-fated villagers—men, women and children—never knew when they might be called upon for the corvée, and have to perform unpaid labour for the State at the cost of health and often life itself. Enjoying abounding prosperity—the evident result of careful administration—the Egyptian people enter upon a new phase in their career with every circumstance in their favour.

The obverse of the ten piastre note is printed in dull green upon light green and yellow, bearing a machined pattern. The reverse is another machined pattern in blue with a lozenge in the centre, containing the majestic seated statues of Memmon, facing, as they have done for century after century, the setting sun.

Owing to the shortage of coin the Indian rupee was made legal tender in Egypt for 6½ piastres; these coins are now being withdrawn from circulation. As the resources of the silver market were available for British coinage, no subsidiary money in base metal was rendered necessary. The currency demands of the Indian Empire (owing to its favourable balance of trade and the prohibition of gold imports on private account) were so enormous, that it was deemed advisable to extend the use of nickel alloy, hitherto applied to the sixteenth and eighth of a rupee, to the quarter and half, but it is worthy of note that the substances of which the subsidiary coinage of the British Empire, its Dominions and Dependencies was composed, practically remained unaffected by war conditions.

The Indian Government, however, issued notes for one and two and a-half rupees, which had an immediate and active circulation, especially in the neighbourhood of the Great Cities of India. This is remarkable, considering how great an innovation is the issue of notes of so small a denomination.

The watermark is identical in each case—a monogram G.R.I. on the left, a five-pointed star in a frame on the right, and a wavy ribbon connecting monogram and frame. The one rupee note has a pink medallion in the centre, and a circular impress of George, King Emperor, fashioned like a coin, on the right. The two and a-half rupee note has a blue medallion in the centre, with green extension of the design on either side. The impress of the King Emperor's head is again on the right, but on this occasion in an octagonal frame. On the top right and the bottom left corners the respective value is set out diagonally.

The main wording is the same in each case: Government of India—I promise to pay the Bearer the sum of   on demand at any Office of Issue.

<p align="center">For the Government of India,
(<i>Here follows signature</i>).</p>

The notes are numbered in the top right and bottom left corners. The reverses have a crown and the Emperor's monogram on the left, and a circle with expressed value on the right. In the centre appears a tablet, which is an epitome of the wonderful realm over which the King Emperor holds sway. Its contents are unique, for the values are set out in eight languages—the principal of the numerous tongues spoken in that great Empire. By the courtesy of an Oriental friend, the following list was compiled:—

1. Urdu . . . Daughter of Persian, spoken all round India.
2. Hindi . . . Daughter of Sanscrit and sister to Urdu, spoken all round India.
3. Maratha . . . Bombay side.
4. Bengali . . . Calcutta side.
5. Oriya . . . Bihar and Orissa.
6. Tamil . . . Deccan language.
7. Teligu . . . Madras language.
8. Gujrati . . . Bombay side.

It is safe to say that since the fall of the Roman Empire no crowned head authority speaks to its subjects in such remarkable diversity of language as does King George.

The one rupee notes are made up into books of 25.

The least satisfactory British emergency paper currency is that issued by the Government of the Straits Settlements. The obverse of the ten cent note is printed in green over a yellow panel centre, upon clumsy white paper, with these words beneath the royal arms :—" The Government of the Straits Settlements promises to pay the bearer on demand at Singapore ten cents (in black) local currency for value received." On the left upper corner within a black circular line is placed " 10 cents." On the left lower corner are Chinese characters (probably the value) and the number, all in black. On the right lower corner is the signature, with the word Treasurer in black, whilst along the right side are placed black characters of some other Eastern language, with the value 10. If the yellow background be carefully examined, the words can be detected " Straits Settlements, ten cents," many times repeated. The reverse of the note is a roughly-executed conventional design in vermilion, in the middle of which is a panel, crown in centre, with Singapore 10$^{c.}$ above and TEN CENTS at foot, together with three small circlets close to the crown carrying the inscription respectively 1–16–17, evidently the date of issue.

The twenty-five cent note is a slightly better production, printed in black upon yellow-lined paper, with a machine design in the middle. A conventional floral border surrounds similar lettering to that upon the ten-cent note. Four black circles occupy the corners; the two upper contain the denomination " 25 " and the two lower " C$^{TS.}$" Inscriptions (tri-lingual) are placed in scrolls at the side and foot. The reverse bears a yellow machined design, surcharged in black with a tiger emerging from the jungle.

Both notes suggest that there must have been considerable danger of forged imitations.

In these days, when Home Rule for Ireland is so much to the fore, it is somewhat of a shock to find that there is an island, part of the British Commonwealth, and close to the shores of the United Kingdom, which possesses the right to issue its own paper currency. The States of Guernsey issued during the Great War excellent notes for five and ten shillings. They are printed in black upon white paper, water-marked with a lozenge containing the local arms. The appearance of each value is similar—a machined frame-like design surrounding an inscription to the following effect :—The States of Guernsey, Guernsey (followed by date, the five shilling specimen in front of the writer is dated 1st September, 1914). Promise to pay the bearer on demand [here follows on the former note five shillings (six francs), on the latter ten shillings (twelve francs)] value received. By authority of the States (here is signature in ink).

The former note has 5s. in the left upper corner and 6 Frs. in the right. In a similar way the latter displays 10s. and 12 Frs. The number is printed on each side of an ornamental coloured centre—red in the former, blue in the latter, note. Opposite to the signature already mentioned is a signature preceded by the abbreviation "Ent[d.]" The reverse of each note bears a handsome machined pattern, in the centre of which is a circle bearing the words : " The States of Guernsey," placed around the arms of Guernsey—three heraldic lions. The colour is again respectively red and blue.

Similar notes were issued for one pound. A strange anomaly that so near home both French and English currency should be legally current, and that pennies should have been counted recently by the baker's dozen !

INDEX.

	PAGE.
Aluminium Coin—French Local	11
Beesley, S. W.—German East African Money	35
Belgian King	41
Bolshevik Finance	65
Brass Coin—Belgian	40
French	11
Swiss	88
British Notes at Archangel	66
Treasury Currency Notes	97
Cardboard Money—Belgian	40, 51
French	15
Chief Cashier—Bank of England	97
Copper Coin—French	15
Darlehenskassen—German	1
Russian	62
Egyptian War Notes	99
French Local Notes	16
Mint Moved	9
Occupied Territory	28
Füssen (German Michael)—50 pf.	30
German East Africa	35
Gold Debased Coin	35
Michael and Dragon (Füssen)	30
Saving Banks	4
Shop Note	7
Typed Note	5
Wit (?)	26, 27, 28
Written Note	6
Guernsey	102
Holland's Hospitality	94
Indian 1 and 2½ Rupee Notes	100
Iron—Danish Coin	88
French Coin	10
German Coin	25
Norwegian Coin	88
Russian Coin	61
Swedish Coin	88
Italian Udine Occupied	76
Japan's Valuable Aid	85
Money—Soviet	65
Montagu, Samuel, & Co.	71

	PAGE.
PRINCE OF PLESS	3
POLAND'S PLIGHT	94
ROMANOFF DYNASTY	61
ROUMANIAN QUEEN'S BRAVERY	79
RUBENS' NOTE	46
SERVIANS MASSACRED	75
SOVIET MONEY	65
STRAITS·SETTLEMENTS	101
SWITZERLAND'S DIFFICULT RÔLE	94
TREASURY CURRENCY NOTES	97
UNITED STATES OF AMERICA	85
VENETIAN TERRITORY OCCUPIED	76
VICTORIA—QUEEN	45
ZINC COIN—BELGIAN	40
FRENCH	11
GERMAN	25

www.ingramcontent.com/pod-product-compliance
Lightning Source LLC
Chambersburg PA
CBHW070548090426
42735CB00013B/3108